SELF-PORTRAIT
IN BLOOM

SELF-PORTRAIT IN BLOOM

by
Niloufar Talebi

l'Aleph

Niloufar Talebi

SELF-PORTRAIT IN BLOOM

2019 Published by l'Aleph – Sweden – www.l-aleph.com

l'Aleph is a Wisehouse Imprint.

ISBN 978-91-7637-563-1

All the translations from the Persian, as well as Paul Éluard's "Air Vif," in this book are by Niloufar Talebi.

"Collective Love" was published in the Catamaran Literary Reader (Summer 2014, No. 7).

The cover image is a version of "Cotton," a digital painting by M. Talebi, the author's father. Cover design by Fatline Studios. http://fatlinestudios.com

This memoir reflects the author's present recollections of experiences over time. Some details, dialogue, and events have been changed, recreated, and condensed.

Translations of Ahmad Shamlou's poetry © 2019 Niloufar Talebi. Translated and published with permission from Aida Shamlou, co-director of the Alef. Bamdad Institute.

Self-Portrait in Bloom © 2019 Niloufar Talebi

For Mahni

who saw me in the fire

and through

"…Language is never innocent…"

—*Roland Barthes*

CONTENTS

Contents	9
Prologue	13
1. Me	19
2. Shamlou	43
3. Aida: Muse, Wife, Assistant, Steward	61
4. Me	65
5. Shamlou	73
6. Me	81
7. The New World	85
8. Tehran	101
9. Shamlou's Funeral	117
10. The Master and Margarita	125
11. San Francisco, My Golden City	133
12. The Birth of a Translator	137
13. A Skyrocketing, 2003–2013	145
14. My Shamlou Projects	147
15. Poems by Ahmad Shamlou	151
Collective Love	153
The Beginning	155
Genesis	157
Nocturne	159
River	160
Poverty	161
Farewell	162
Unfinished Ghazal…	164
Song of Acquaintance	165
You and I…	166
Aida in the Mirror	168
Nocturne	171
On the Winter Within	172
The One Who Says I Love You	174
I Wish I Were Water	175
Hamlet	177
Nelson Mandela	180

An Epic?   181
Dark Song   182
The Anthem of Abraham in Flames   183
Rupture   187
Funeral Address   189
In the Moment   190
Still Life   191
Grappling with Silence   192
Nocturne   199
Epitaph   200
Birth   201
At the Threshold   202
I Cannot Not Be Beautiful   206
16. Venom of Snake   207
17. To Colleague, My Censor   219
18. Time, a Long, Long, Time (Through the Fire)   233
19. Blossomfield   237
CODA   243
Notes 250
References 252
Illustrations 254
Acknowledgments 255
About Ahmad Shamlou 256

There are two books in this book. One portrait of me and one of Ahmad Shamlou. And they intersect.

PROLOGUE

Memory is fiction.
Flash fragments.

There is no exact equivalent in English for the Persian word *zahre-maar*, at least none that I've thought up, but the literal translation is "venom of snake." *Zahr*/venom, *e*/of, *maar*/snake. Three distinct syllables.

I love the way the word sounds, how the Z can be emphasized, *ZZZZAH!*, how the H can be guttural—no, not as the Arabic H that veers into KH, we're talking a breathy H, as in a hardy Hi!—before the release into the elongated AA, *MAAAAAAAR*, like a snake itself.

Zahre-maar has multiple meanings depending on context and delivery. As an exclamatory phrase, *Zahre-maar!* can be a bitter response to someone, a retort for being wronged, but it could also be delivered with a lighter touch, feigning a greater degree of hurt than felt. For jest.

Zahre-maar reminds me of a board game I used to play with my brother, *Maar O Pelleh*, Snakes and Ladders. Each player competes to be the first to arrive at the final square by rolling dice and advancing on a board. On the way, each could randomly encounter ladders (which give a leg up) or snakes (the opposite). If a player lands on the Envy box, for example, the snake of envy drops the player to only the second of usually one hundred squares in some games. Forward momentum seriously thwarted.

Zahre-maar can also be used with the auxiliary verbs *shodan*, to become, or *kardan*, to do:

Zahre-maaram shod = It was ruined for me.
Zahre-maaram kard = Someone ruined it for me.

To ruin something for someone.

Yeki bood, yeki nabood.
Once upon a time
there was one, there was none*
which was not the negation of one
but its own being
misunderstood
yearning   to   break   free

Upon creation, there was one and the polar opposite of one. One was angel, infinity, existence, fulfillment, light, oneness, and the other was the equal opposite, merely a shadow, where light wasn't, where nothing was, an absence, nothing, zero. Then, the equal opposite objected! What could possibly be more unequal than one versus zero, all versus none? it said. This is not an equal opposite, it is a ghastly manifestation of the question. And thus, to make the playing field even, was born JUSTICE. The shadow, the none, was given the value of negative or minus one, which is in itself a futile concept, there existing no negative in reality. But it simply had to be imagined and created to make the game equal, so it could unfold in the first place.

1. ME

I BEGAN WRITING THIS BOOK decades ago, and I have already rewritten it a thousand times over, erasing and recasting the past as I went and now go—a past ungraspable like the iridescence of an oil spill. Many selves of mine have come and gone and have yet to come. I have high expectations of my future selves. I want one of them to live with lions. Another to be a seducer of sculptors' hands. Still another to backpack the wilderness alone. A discoverer of uncharted lands. An Egyptian actress in the Alexandria of Agatha Christie. Jeanne d'Arc. A grande dame, a doyenne with doting admirers seeing her through old age.

In a sense, I began writing my life as it was unfolding, or rather, seeing it through the lens of literature. When I was getting away with pranks in school, I thought I was a hero, funny. Later, as I recalled it, I marveled at the spirited girl who was leading. Now, I see that people don't want to let others get away with being themselves because they themselves do not have the moxie to. I hung around my outsiders' circle in college and wailed against "society" that owed us so much. Of our band of outraged, bohemian bosom buddies, one completely abdicated from society, as Susan Sontag put it, living without a phone in a hellish desert, another is a bar pianist in Paris playing for chanteuses, actualizing our "Lost Generation" idyll.

Time flows. New strata of me deposit onto the erased me. My life is alluvial.

This self-portrait, one slice of infinitely curated Creation Stories of me, is captured in print before its erasure. Therefore, it is fiction. But the Truth. A perfectly manicured chocolate cake that is not also a carrot cake or a cheesecake. Nor lemon meringue.

Let's see if we can trace it all back to the mysterious origins of me, Tortured Artist.

I have no one to blame but myself.

For most of my life, I have felt unworthy.

I thought, or was made to feel, that I was bad. There was from me some expectation of domesticity, because I was born girl. I do not mean I come from the overt kind of patriarchal, honor-killing, Middle Eastern family you might be imagining right about now. No, our brand of patriarchy was more invisible. We are modernized, even Westernized. But herein lies the problem: Misogyny is embedded within Westernized societies that shrewdly deny their own kind of patriarchy, instead pointing fingers to the "barbaric" societies of the East they denigrate in order to colonize.

Being an artist, I betrayed the unspoken expectation of immigrant children—to restore the loss, repay the sacrifices made toward a better life for me in the new world. I think I have failed at this. The burden of this guilt exhausts me.

I backed out of so much. Children. Bourgeoisie. Casual friendships. Being generally "normal." All in order to write. I bump against my marital life, which provides me with the sustenance necessary to write because I simply cannot swallow the framework that prescribes a specific role from me. (House)Wife.

Even as a full-blown adult, the act I show my father is largely a *Theater of Good Wifery.* It's just easier not to debate when I am told I should be taking care of my husband, making him dinner. The taking-care-of-each-other advice goes both ways, but somehow it feels as if the bondage of domesticity is being passed down to *me.*

I have painted myself into one corner and one corner only.

So you see, I have no one to blame but myself. I was born girl. I became immigrant. I am artist. What the hell else did I expect?

They say that every new work of art redefines all those that came before it, offering a new reading of them, reorganizing them anew in the continuum of our collective imaginations.

Scientists say that each time we recall a memory, it loses fidelity.

Fidelity defined: *The quality or state of being faithful; accuracy in details; the degree to which an electronic device (as a record player, radio, or television)*—surely also the electric brain—*accurately reproduces its effect (as sound or picture).*

So we erase each time we remember. Each new recall, each new version then overrides and rewrites the past. "ours truths"

Erosion. Sedimentation. Ad infinitum.

Tehran, Iran, 1976 — Everything starts with this image burned into my memory: the back of a schoolgirl standing at her blue bedroom's window watching snowfall. She writes four succinct lines in a notebook that is now lost. Somehow she *knows* this is poetry.

I saw all the whites in the sky, I saw them pile into bulging mounds on branches, I saw solitary flakes melt at the windowsill, I saw the throbbing silence of snowfall, I saw trees stripped to their elements, I saw their stillness and the stirrings beneath the frozen earth, I saw a hushed city, I saw the earnestness in my young parents' tasks, I saw multitudes and beauty, I saw rivers stream down Mount Damavand, I saw another dimension, forces beyond the known, I saw the unspoken, I saw the mother, I saw the weight and the weightlessness of things, I saw time suspended, I saw the eternal.

already solitary
voyager

                    whispers rose up in me

when I was eight
a feeling overcame

                    from watching silent snowfall

and   a poem was born
in my notebook
covered in black plastic

                    with diamond holograms

four
succinct lines
simple
perfect.

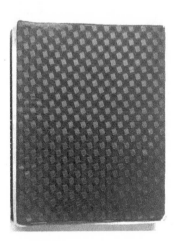

Silence is an animal with two faces:

1.   Voluntary silence
        Silence to breathe
        Silence into the labyrinth of the self
        Silence to cleanse
        Silence to undo and exorcise
        Silence, that buffer between bodies

First born: London, England.
First birthday photo: dressed in a dirndl.
Perched at grandfather's chest
mommy's doll is stuffed
into white lacy tights that leave
their impression
on her Michelin Man legs.

Shuttled between Tehran and London
and Hamburg and Sunderland
the toddler is said to have
stopped crying
engrossed when placed in
                                          front of the telly
with Tom Jones
singing and gyrating
his hips.

First momentous memory: possessed
jumping on a spare bed in the cool storage room
chanting, *I have a peepee, I have a peepee.*

The child's make-believe world
in her blue bedroom
is a cozy bed encased
in a glossy, kelly green frame
an arcade of dreams
a pilgrim's boat
its perimeter the frontier

separating shelter

and the vast ocean

of sharks and bogeymen beyond.

The all-night game: all limbs must stay strictly within the frame, or else the beyond, the savage beyond.

Next door a little brother sleeps, his toy soldiers poised on battlefields.

Mommy dressed me at her closet of wonders and scents in a green polyester costume with flouncy sleeves she had sewn for my role as "leaf" in a kindergarten show. Or so I remembered for decades. Recently, a woman writes me saying she was my elementary school classmate. I try to find her name familiar, convincing myself that I do, as we do with so many fellow countrymen's names that may or may not belong in our pasts. She mentions our "flower" play in elementary school.

Clank clank clank in Mommy's heels down the hall when I am home alone…

Breathless from bliss on a tricycle.

Twirling my short pleated skirts
in front of the gramophone,
dancing with wrists bent, hands blooming magnolias.

Mommy makes snacks of steamed fava beans and red beets and turnips
on dark winter afternoons.

A groovy, young father's navy blue BMW 2002 with its bunny
wabbit grill.

Velvet and wool blankets heaped over a low table we sat around, a
heating unit housed under it, our legs jutting into the heated cubby, a
toasty *korsi* on winter nights of soups and stews and writing between the
lines.

Every school textbook opened with full-page headshots of the Shah and
Empress Farah.

Sleeping in a girls dormitory for a summer where my bed is once
covered end to end in sand, maybe from the beaches of the English
Channel nearby, and my dolls are dismembered, and we hear rumors of
a savage murder in the woods surrounding the international boarding
school, but no one tells my parents back in Tehran and neither do I
because I am somehow mute.

Barbie and Sindy dolls and their seasonal wardrobes and tiny plastic high-
heeled shoes. Sindy's lavender royal cape, purchased in Bath, United
Kingdom. My love for shades of purple unmistakable even early on.

Riding a glittery gold bicycle on the grounds of the apartment complex
around a large swimming pool downstairs from my blue bedroom.

An older, sensible father's blue Peugeot 504 and its backseat booster seat.

A turquoise and elongated ceramic figure, a mysterious seated feline, nestled on the shelves of my father's office, a sprawling city where I run laps and get eye exams.

Dolphin diving in the pool in my red one-piece suit either holding my nose or wearing a pinkish, flesh-colored nose clip. Marco. Polo. Always with the fear of *Jaws*. Until dusk when we rush home shuddering, wrapped in our towels, lips blue and teeth chattering.

Too early, it was too early to cry each night into the pillow, too early to have begun fearing my parents' abandonment of me. The death-fear that enters us at birth and propels us into our actions. Every church thrashing, every sports-arena roar, every holler of joy is to defy, delay the inescapable.

Reciting memorized poetry before the entire class as early as the first grade.

Multi-family trips to orchards in remote villages where one family or another owns land, *zameen*, in Karaj and other villages around Tehran. I begin to see the ruthless pecking order among children. Four, even two years apart was an unbridgeable valley then.

My generous surgeon father's patients from near and far bear gifts of gratitude. Live turkeys we kept in our winter-emptied pool in the white house from the peasant patients, and Beluga caviar by the tin cans from the affluent.

A train ride to vacation at the Caspian Sea in the northern, subtropical region of Iran with the same families, physician colleagues of my father. It seemed as if we had taken over all the cars, a feast of parents standing, holding on to poles and children underfoot, weaving between pants and skirts, the anticipation of sun, sand, and beach in every cell of our bodies. Pickled garlic, *mooseer*, served with fresh fish only makes sense in that climate.

Lying on my stomach on the car's backseat from a first-degree sunburn during the drive home through windy, mountainous roads connecting the Caspian Sea to Tehran.

Back home after the walks in the moist woods of the north, an itch at the base of my neck just inside my hairline. A tick fattens there—not of the Lyme variety. A doctor at my father's clinic pops it off with pincers.

Hiking the mountains surrounding Tehran. My father so comfortable on those slopes. Stopping to breakfast on wooden structures built atop brawling streams flowing down the slopes. We sit at the wooden banquettes to have fried eggs, *nimroo*, tea, fresh-baked bread and farmer's or feta cheese, and little bags of cheese puffs for the kids, inhaling that early morning mountain air. The breakfast everyone still tastes. There's a feeling of freedom, endless possibility. We are in a film of entirely different people captured in silent and scratchy black-and-white celluloid. I was born with my father's long legs. We are mountain goats, he and I, hiking the steep foothills of the Alborz mountain range north of Tehran, capped by the mighty Damavand peak.

Ever since the 1979 Iranian revolution was declared "victorious," and one year of chaos had ensued as the Ayatollah Khomeini was digging his claws into government, schools had been gender-segregated, and *hejab*, women covering their heads and bodies, made mandatory. It was easy to hide one's mouth discreetly holding the tail end of a scarf over it. I had just returned from the United States, where my father had sent my mother, brother, and me to take refuge while the bloody uprising was taking its course. I re-enrolled in the same school where I had spent my beloved elementary years, *Ettefagh*, the Jewish school across the street from Tehran University.

There, while in junior high, when a teacher was absent, as class monitor I corralled a classroom of sixty girls sitting by the threes in rows and columns of wooden benches like lines in an I Ching hexagram. We carved so many names into them. I took my stage at the blackboard and entertained with ad hoc performances of making faces, putting on voices, and any other shenanigan or skit that came to body. I could keep the class in stitches for the hour-long period. Which vice principal could object? No unruliness, no strays running down the hall.

Later, at another school, from my back-row bench I orchestrated a class of fifty high school girls. Their periodic *moo*ing out of unmoving mouths drove the teacher to tears. Incapable of taking control of her classroom, she pulled me out of class, being that I was the straight-A class monitor, and implored that I find the ringleader.

I also mobilized the spitting of orange-peel pellets onto the blackboard. The tip of Bic pens that had been hollowed of their ink cartridges were punched into orange peel, pellets were lodged in and fired at the blackboard with a swift blow into the other end of the casing when the teacher was chalking the board.

On summer afternoons that stretched for eons, I retreated into Hemingway and Farrokhzad and de Chateaubriand and Gertrude Stein and Behrangi and Dickens and Emma Goldman and Al-Ahmad and

Neruda and Fuentes and García Márquez and Daneshvar and Twain in my cool bedroom sanctuary. My father would, upon leaving home for the clinic in the morning, hand me a book—not picture books, we are talking Kafka—and tell me we were discussing it in the evening when he returned. And such went my literary education, and all the personas that I got to take on when immersed in those other worlds, intimate with so many characters and their dramas.

Nothing was missed from the absence of religious faith in my home. We had literature. My parents found spiritual solace in art. I would come to understand that the making of art promised that all my travails would be in the service of something better, building toward a redemption, giving my life an arc bent toward meaning.

During all the years I lived in Iran both before and after the revolution, I exchanged heaps of hand-written letters in English with pen pals all over the world. There were readily available forms I cannot remember how or through whom to be filled out and sent away that resulted magically in pen pal matches. I wonder whether children still practice this mysterious exchange, or whether internet connectivity hijacked this pleasure. Letters would arrive from faraway places in exotic or thin blue *Par Avion* envelopes bearing unfamiliar stamps and ink charting journeys through ports. I carefully lifted the stamps to add to my heavy stamp-collector's book that was filled with picturesque stamps from my father's correspondences from abroad and others he bought my brother and me at stamp stores, another favorite childhood token lost in emigration. I don't have copies of the letters I wrote, nor any trace of where, to whom, and how many were sent. So many lost Creation Stories. Perhaps somewhere in my musty storage bags filled with letters received from my Iranian schoolmates after I left might be lodged an odd copy.

Packets of Pop Rocks arrived from America. The most memorable flavor: purple grape. I had never put anything like them in my mouth. Purely chemical tiny rocks unexpectedly thudding into the upper palate of my mouth. Almost violent.

What is time?

— A way of keeping track of how things evolve. The order of one thing coming after another.

— Causality. What causes what.

— A human construct, time may or may not exist.

— Everything may have already happened, and we are just aware of little pieces at a time.

— A way to ensure everything does not happen at once.

— Space is a way to ensure that not everything happens to *us*.

— A standard argument for time running forward:

We remember the past and not the future.

And what if we were going backwards in time?

We would progressively forget the past, undoing memories we have formed.

— We can time-travel into the past and the future:

We remember the first kiss and imagine next month's vacation.

— People with dementia cannot imagine themselves fully or make new memories or predict the future. Our memories are crucial to our identities.

— Time feels longer if we are present. Time flies if we are busy.

I felt this during my car accident when all my attention went to that one thing, the swerving of my car across many lanes of the 405 freeway traffic toward the median at high speed while singing at the top of my lungs to Yma Sumac playing loudly on the stereo. My whole life did not flash before my eyes, but I did make a curious decision, or rather, the decision presented itself to me: I was moving to San Francisco—which I did on a Monday in December 1994, the day my physical therapy for broken bones ended. I had $60 in my pocket and no job, only a carry-on with a portable laptop and printer. When I was put onto a stretcher at the scene of the accident, I directed the paramedics to retrieve the master copy of a documentary I had made and was delivering to its producer from the glove box of the totaled car. I think of the accident as a not-so-gentle nudge to stop moping directionless at my parents' home after college and to get my life going already.

Our experience of time distorted, we are visited by moments, tableaus. We attribute different degrees of importance to them by storing and dramatizing certain episodes, rendering them integral to our essence and being. Our sense of self is a game of Russian roulette.

While reaching back in time, I searched the internet for old images of my schools. Every time, I type the name of the school of my hearts, Ettefagh.

My mother was so exacting about my education that she would enroll me at the beginning of each school year in a name school that promised the moon: the American school, the French school among them. She would interrogate me every day after school to get to the bottom of how the day was structured, gauge if I had learned enough, and how much homework I had. Sure enough, no school ever passed muster, and two weeks into the school year, and a whole new school uniform to buy, I would return to Ettefagh, a public school with a reputation for high academic standards. In addition to being closed on Fridays, the Sabbath in Iran, Ettefagh school was also closed on Saturdays, following Jewish

Sabbath, which was normally the first day of the week in Iran. I grew up with an unusual two-day weekend. To make up for the lost time, our school days were long, 8 a.m.–4 p.m. with a full load of academic classes. My arms were weighed down by a heavy leather bag of textbooks and notebooks, including ones with black nylon covers with a hologram design. I loved the time at the end of summer when we shopped for new school supplies. I loved choosing which notebook for which subject, writing my name in them with my favorite four-color pens in my well-practiced and eye-pleasing handwriting, keeping everything neat. At home I settled at my desk for several hours of homework each night. The endurance.

People just like me had posted their old photographs. Others had found vintage video clips, captioning them with nostalgic notes: *Does anyone remember this? Our beloved school!*

I looked hard into those black-and-white or faded images and shaky sepia clips for *something*. Anything—the window of my first grade class where I learned the letters A, B, and D in the first phrase we learn at school, *Baba ahb dahd. Father water gave.* The wide windows of the lunch hall where I would take my little first-grader brother's hand after anxiously looking for him among the hundreds of uniformed, unleashed children running erratically like atoms under heat in the school yard, where we would haul our large, insulated, black lunch thermoses lovingly stacked with our mother's homemade foods to eat together. My brother would not remember later that I cared for him like a worried mother.

I need pieces of the past to help me move forward. I pore over old photographs, images that enthrall me endlessly. I depend on them to live. They are frozen yet never stilted to my eyes. Private gazes into scenes summon shadows of memories, memories that are reverse engineered, manufactured from the photographs and mistaken, stored, and embedded as real memories. Each time I look at or think of them they animate whole fictions, myths that are more ancient and modern versions than the myths they conjure. While many fragments recede, some fragments magnify to become primitive symbols of my fears and drives. I redescribe their implications through my own experience. These myths are personal and sacred not because they are flights into an imagined antiquity, or remembrances of beauty, but because they express to me something real in myself, something ungraspable to me through other means, what fulfills a dim longing to belong to a greater sense.[1]

In these images, I looked for scale. Was that really the entrance that I went through every day? Where was the grand hallway through which my glamorous mother would strut like a movie star in her long fur coat to fetch me? Was it in reality a dingy corridor? Was she really wearing fur? Was what I imagined as the gilded gateway to Constantinople or some other rich, ancient city only a dilapidated and unused iron gate to the forlorn ramp next to the playground? Was that the temple with the high ceilings I would visit each morning before class, that endless field-maze of platforms and tables and podiums and Torahs we played hide-and-seek through? Where was that football field of a playground at the end of which the tastiest, greasy, chocolate donuts we called *pirashki*, and *negrokees*—chocolate-covered marshmallow treats—were sold from a low, gated portal in the wall? How far down the street was the stationery store with the puffy stickers, glitter, and designer erasers that smelled of fruits and bubble gum that I would sniff in sustained inhalations and even put in my mouth, they were so enticing.

We pronounced the name for the marshmallow treats as one word, *negrokees,* like *necropolis,* not realizing the Latin roots and racist reference of *Negro kiss.* The only black people I had seen were my African nanny and her husband. I only know this because I saw a photograph of them with my family on the occasion of their daughter's birthday. I was a newborn. We were still in England. My petite young mother next to the large husband in native garb. I don't know which country in Africa. In another photograph, my nanny, a nurse in the hospital where my father received his ophthalmology fellowship, is holding me on her lap, and my mother is standing behind her chair gazing at me in adoration with a craned neck. In Iran, I played with Jewish and Christian children in the same apartment complex, in the same school yards. I was exposed.

We peer so deeply into images of lost places and times for a hint of meaning as to who we were. We hope to superimpose our ghosts onto these spaces to make an imaginary film of our days, but the discrepancy between what we think was and what really was as we yearn to bridge in some way to what is lost, evaporated into another dimension of time, is our actual lives.

I once stood in a circle of other ten-year-olds, many of them well-toned Arab boys in tight designer jeans and shiny belts and crisp shirts and turbans, who took my fellow boarding-school mate, a blue-eyed, blond-haired Greek girl with honey skin who looked like our image of a Biblical angel, and passed her around and pummeled her inside the circle.

We were in a secluded part of the grounds near the woods. It was a misty summer by the southern sea of the English Channel. Five or six boys beating one girl. I remember freezing, staring dumbfounded. Before I knew it, the young-man-handling and assault was over.

Even early on I knew this was a Terror of Beauty—
which I later read about in Rilke's *Duino Elegies*.

Beauty is only
> *the first touch of terror*
>> *we can still bear* [2]

The violence against me had not started then.

Not yet...

Decades earlier, in 1931, a boy of six, a future poet with the pen name Alef Bamdad, meaning A. Dawn or A. Daybreak, witnessed the bloody public lashing of a lowly soldier. A feeling overcame him, he said, and he *knew*.

He wrote:

I am Daybreak, in the end
weary

…

I was six the first time I laid eyes
upon grief-stricken Abel receiving
a whipping from himself
public ceremony
in full befitting swing:
there was a row of soldiers, a pageant of cold,
silent chess pawns,
the glory of a dancing colorful flag
trumpets blasting and the life-consuming
rapping of drums
so Abel would not ail from the sound
of his own sobbing.[3]

When I was ten, around the disorienting time my body started to exist for me, I also became aware of my country. Iran was having a revolution, shedding its oppressive monarchy.

We left for the United States in 1978 and returned in 1979, a few months after the revolution was declared "victorious" with the Shah of Iran fleeing to Egypt, not knowing, as no one did, what we were returning to.

What unfolded over the following four and only other years I lived in Iran: chaotic arrests and disappearances, martial law, half of the brutal eight-year war with Iraq, violently enforced, compulsory *hejab*, the denouncement of alcohol, neckties, beardless faces, and anything "Western," watching what you said in public—anyone could be a spy, even the girl sitting next to you in class. Poor, angry, young men promised their comeuppance by the Ayatollah became the Iranian Revolutionary Guard Corps, *Pasdaran*, armed with machine guns and beige Toyota Land Cruisers—seeing them still makes me double over with nausea—patrolling the streets with carte blanche to stop, arrest, confiscate, imprison, rape, kill. The birth of a religious dictatorship centuries in the making. And a mass exodus of which my family was a part.

And meeting Shamlou.

The poet, Ahmad Shamlou, also known as Alef Bamdad.

Iran underwent two pivotal events in the twentieth century regarding women and their dress.

The first was *kashfe-hejab*, the forced *un*veiling of women decreed by Reza Shah in 1935, the founder of the short-lived Pahlavi dynasty, a welcome decree by the Westernized upper classes, but traumatic for women whose covering was intimately connected with their religious devotion and identity, leaving them exposed, despondent. This fed the alienation between the clergy and the monarchy, causing clashes at various points throughout the century until the deposition of Reza Shah's son, the Shah of Iran, in 1979.

The second was the forceful veiling of Iranian women imposed by the clergyman Ayatollah Khomeini's new, brutal regime, usurped from the hands of the many factions that played a part in overthrowing the Pahlavi dynasty, "winning" the 1979 revolution.

The Ayatollah's strong-arm men, the *Pasdaran,* were a motley band, sons of the underclass promised their rightful place in the revolutionary rhetoric. Their families had suffered in the margins of a society dominated by the British and the Americans, in turn priding itself for being modernized, Westernized, leaving behind tribal people, peasants, crafts people, denying them the upward mobility their exploitation provided the modernized and urban bourgeois class. These young men were recruited in the name of *Allah,* and with blanket power they exercised to take out their decades-long revenge upon the corrupt ruling class. And terrorize they did, breaking any and all rules, for it was the rule of chaos, unaware that they were mere pawns, strong-arms for yet another despotic regime that would soon forget them as well. Their violence included deflowering maidens upon arrest, justified by a self-serving interpretation of some likely falsified Koranic verse that no virgin could be killed. They were to be addressed as *brother.*

Once, I was dallying on the sidewalk with my mother and brother, waiting for my father to park and join us for our dentist visit, when they closed in, the *brothers.* Out of nowhere, cars including the domestic car, *Paykan*—not dissimilar to Soviet-era national cars—sped and screeched at our feet. Young men slinging machine guns leapt out.

The next thing I remember is all three of us on our knees. My ten-year-old brother's silky prepubescent hair in a cascading bowl cut shimmered under the winter sun. The next snapshot is of my father, his gloves or wallet in both of his hands clasped in front of him as he usually carried things. What a scene to walk into. He argues with the *brothers* who would not be reasoned with, for they are not in the business of justice for the class that, as far as they are concerned, has thrived on the backs of their parents. Then, my brother, my father, and I are in the back seat of the *Paykan,* my father in the middle. The young man in charge is in the passenger seat addressing the windshield. My mother is standing outside probably with a gun pointing at her. Other guards are loitering around their own cars. The *brother* in charge has been to the front to fight in the Iran-Iraq war. My father, too, as a medical doctor serving for two months each year. The *brother* has had an injury that still looms. My father is able to give *brother* the medical advice he so needs. *Brother* lets us go with a warning.

Apparently a few wisps of my hair were hanging loose out of the new contraption in my life, my headscarf. This was Tehran in 1983.

2. SHAMLOU

A HMAD **SHAMLOU WAS BORN** on December 12, 1925, by his own account on a bleak and cold snowy day in a spiritless house at 134 *Safi Alishah* road in Tehran, Iran. What is believed to have been his birth home seems to be standing abandoned in a country that barely allows gatherings of fans making a pilgrimage to his graveside on the anniversary of his passing on Sunday, July 23, 2000.

I was awaited in a bleak house
by the sacred mirrored fountain
near the mystic's temple.
(Perhaps why
I found the shadow of Satan
staking me out
from the outset).

At age five
I was still despondent from the unthinkable blow of my own birth
and grew up rootless
on salty sand
to the grunting of a drunk camel and the ghostly presence
of poisonous reptiles in a dust-bowl more remote
than the dusty memory of the last row of date palms
on the fringes of the last dry river.[4]

Shamlou's father was an itinerant military officer whose assignments took his family to far-flung corners of Iran—then still called Persia—exposing the young Shamlou to the peoples, tribes, languages, folklore and customs, and the harsh realities of a nation teetering at the edge of modernity and ravaged by feudalist class warfare at the hands of weak monarchs. First, of the Qajar dynasty who ruled from 1789 to 1925, and later, the Pahlavi dynasty who ruled from 1925–1979, gradually diminishing Iran in size and power as they gave away land and assets to foreign states.

At the turn of the twentieth century, the increasing exchange between the Persian intelligentsia and the rapidly shifting European states had resulted in cultural and political shifts. Persia underwent a Constitutional Revolution between 1905 and 1911, which led to the establishment of a parliament, *Majles*.

Shamlou's birth year, 1925, was the pivotal year when Reza Khan, a military man, seized the throne and declared himself king, *Shah*, founding the Pahlavi dynasty. In his vision of modernization, Reza Shah enforced the *un*veiling of women, *kashfe-hejab,* and in 1935, changed the country's name on the roster of nations from "Persia" to "Iran," the name of the country in the Persian language itself (endonym), and a variant of "Aryan," a self-designation by the Indo-Iranian people, later distorted during World War II toward atrocities in the name of racial ideology.

Shamlou spent an unhappy childhood in various provincial towns witnessing much misery and suffering around him. He recalled scenes of this desolate childhood, his external realities, in *Keyhan-e Sal* magazine: In the city of Kash, he saw a starving Baluchi boy on a mattress that he had soiled the previous night, likely from the terror of impending death in a filthy boardinghouse. He remembered the agonizing sight of a sickly teacher and his stomach-churning lash marks in the city of Mashhad. There were villages without trees for respite from the searing sun, fields without water. The tears of his mother washing with her own hands the dead body of her son, Shamlou's brother.

When Shamlou was a young boy, he overheard a young neighbor play the piano, maybe Chopin. He experienced "the first undefinable sensations of puberty: a blend of pleasure and pain, death and rebirth, and who knows what else." He decided there and then what he wanted to do with his life. But he was given no music lessons, even taunted. Shamlou mused later that his poetry arose from his stifled longing for music in the same way that the dance-like designs of Persian carpets (and calligraphy) harbored in them the indigenous Persian desire for dance and song, long suppressed under Islam, which swept through Persia in the seventh century.

There was a silence to Shamlou's childhood. With no one to talk to, no one to stoke his imagination, he turned inward, into the well of his own self.

The itinerant life of Shamlou's family meant an interrupted education, transferring schools, and being held back. In high school, Shamlou left for Tehran, but ultimately abandoned school altogether. The image of Cain beating Abel was the door to another world for him. He diverted his attention to reading and literature, his interests spanning politics to poetry.

Around this time, Iran was in the throes of the 1941 Anglo-Russian invasion of Iran, which was to force the opening of a supply route for Russian forces. Shamlou became briefly involved with Iran's communist party, the *Hezbeh Tudeh,* or the Tudeh Party of Iran, literally, the party of the masses. His early political activities led to a momentary mix-up in a nationalist tendency in Iran that temporarily fell on the side of the Axis powers and against the Allies. He was arrested in Tehran and transferred to a Russian Red Army prison in Rasht, where he spent twenty-one months, and finally released in the fall of 1944.

Soon after, in 1945, Shamlou's father was transferred to the northwestern state of Azerbaijan in Iran, and their home was raided by the guerrilla forces of the democratic faction. Shamlou and his father were held blindfolded before a firing squad for two hours before a last-minute reprieve.

Shamlou's domiciles were raided throughout his life, his manuscripts burned and stolen, confiscated works he tried to recreate from memory while plotting new ones. Sometimes he went into hiding. He began to realize that his voice could not be expressed by aligning with any political ideologies or parties or stealthily pasting protest posters in the middle of the night. Writing would be his only work, nothing would be as potent as his pen, nothing large enough to contain him. Shamlou transforms from an outward activist to introspective witness.

When Shamlou launched into his literary career in the fertile period after World War II, Persian poetry had been remolded and given a new dynamism. His coming of age and evolution as a free spirit in an increasingly unfree Iranian society posed a challenge, but he managed to reflect his social and humanistic ideals in his work. The reformist spirit of the time was reflected in the works of socially motivated poets preceding him. Poets such as Bahar, Iraj, Dehkhoda, Farrokhi, Eshghi, and Lahuti played key roles in this process of freeing Persian poetry from the state of decline and stagnation it had fallen into. The florid language of the nineteenth century had alienated the masses and led to the gradual isolation of the ruling classes from the realities of life. Classical imagery with its metaphors wrapped in candles and moths and taverns and lady wine-bearers no longer reflected the concerns of the citizens of a bold, new century.

In their wake came the poet Nima Yushij, born Ali Esfandiari in 1897 in Yush in the northern province of Mazandaran, and largely referred to as Nima. In his rustic simplicity, Nima cloistered himself at home for twenty years as he single-handedly challenged traditionalist tendencies in Iranian poetry, namely its subjects and metrical forms, and began to update the language of poetry in the language of his time, all against a barrage of criticism for upsetting tradition. His work was denounced for not even being written in the Persian language. Progress was slow—with each new publication he took one step forward and two steps back. In 1945, Nima was a renegade star, but in only five years he would turn into a sun around which rotated a galaxy. He would be a vanguard, cementing his *She're No,* or New Poetry movement.

After abandoning high school, Shamlou began working in a bookstore. Soon after, his first volume of poetry, *Forgotten Songs* (1947), was published, what he later considered a workbook of his classically influenced poems. Reading one of Nima's poems, *"Knell"*—on the first day of spring, no less—transformed Shamlou's vision of the potential of poetry. Shamlou would track down Nima's address and knock on his door, where appeared a man who resembled drawings Shamlou had seen of Nima. Shamlou introduces himself and expresses his intentions to apprentice under the poet. Nima found in the serious young poet an ally in his vision. In his zeal, Shamlou visited Nima almost every day, never taking into account that he might be imposing on Nima's time.

Shamlou became Nima's champion, publishing Nima's seminal poem, *"Afsaneh"* (*"Myth"*) in 1950. In the same year, Shamlou published his pivotal poem, *"To the Red Blossom of a Shirt,"* in which metric language was disregarded, the poem heralding the free verse revolution—known as *She're Sepid,* meaning white verse—that Shamlou would engineer.

Shamlou later recalled, *In the beginning, when we young poets were composing non-metrical, non-rhyming poetry, many of the elders, who were terrified of innovation, disinclined to accept these new forms, used our work against us, called us inexperienced, repudiated our work of not being poetry. But why? we would ask, and they would mock us:* You are so uneducated and foolish that you don't even realize what you've written is prose!

But Shamlou pressed on experimenting with language. He harnessed the healing powers of poetry as his weapon against tyranny, his tool for connecting with a larger public. Shamlou's worldview matured. He educated himself on a robust regimen of international literatures, gaining independence of thought. He imagined himself in a lineage of writers he considered friends across time and language, a collective that created the blueprints for our humanity.

No one in my family remembers how we came to host Shamlou in our home. During the literary gatherings, which in my mind were wild artists' salons, Shamlou was the centerpiece everyone deferred to, his mastery of language and history and culture so superseded everyone else's that there was no questioning him. Only sitting at the feet of the titan. Other literary heavyweights joining us included Gholam-Hossein Saedi, in whose apartment I would later see a large poster of Beethoven above the entrance staircase, and who would disappear from time to time and when let out of prison, where he was beaten with electrical cables and his mouth pried open to take his torturer's piss—which he told us about while howling and as casually as, *Where is your bathroom*— would resume spirited socializing as before. These people were not new to torture for literature, I thought, my mind already racing with fuzzy torture scenarios I had no business imagining at such a young age, gleaned from our guests and the books I was handed to read about the torture of political prisoners in South America. Torture of female body parts I could not comprehend. Having to witness unspeakable torture of my parents was a nightmare that haunts me still.

We were not allowed to tell anyone about our visitors. The threat of surveillance loomed in those uncertain years. Every one of our loud and musical salons was susceptible to a sudden raid, a knocking down of the door and barging in of half a dozen armed *brothers* to loot, arrest. But so far as I know, Shamlou turned out to be too big to touch, even if he was critical of the new regime, which he considered to be nothing short of a handoff of despotic power from one group to another. In the summer of 1979, he wrote in the weekly journal, *Tehran in Images*:

The regular programming, sunrise, has been canceled without further notice. Ravens are approaching to occupy this entire realm. Terrible news is impending, but the ravens will not bear good tidings.

Shamlou was one of the most visible and written-about artist-activists of his time, rising to the charge of his time. Some have argued that had Shamlou not been possessed by charisma, he might not otherwise have achieved his icon-like status with a cult-like following. He was a

Jean-Paul Sartre's 1947 essays on *engagement*, or commitment, spawned a global movement in the literary discourse of ensuring that literature would serve the struggle for liberation. Sartre believed that words were actions, and that a writer could influence history through writing. Sartre dismissed autonomous writing—"art for art's sake"—as an invention of nineteenth century bourgeois authors. *Engagement* was writing in the service of liberation.

Similarly, Shamlou developed his own call to arms, a brand of socially engaged commitment, *ta'ahhod* in Persian, which peaked in the decades before the Iranian revolution. Shamlou's poetics called upon the collective of human beings to strive for a meaningful and utopian kind of liberation. The idea that the world could be changed by the power of literature was exciting in the 1950s. Shamlou was a Humanist in the sense that he took humanity as the center of a universe, and modern poetry as the grounds for expressing the ideal that people should be free and construct their own destinies. So crucial was freedom to Shamlou that he never stopped advocating for it:

Searching for success, prosperity, and happiness is futile unless people are absolutely free. But people are not even relatively free, so they cannot be happy. A person who is in the bondage of laws, rules, duties, attachments, dependencies, and their own conscience, struggling to satisfy other people's greed and lust, will inevitably lose all of his or her creativity and will mistake the advancements of technology as his or her own when in fact that person is nothing more than a cog in the wheel of those machines. So, of what use is freedom to this person?

Humanity and human culture will only ever blossom in the context of freedom. But as long as prejudice reigns, society will suffocate. Humans rise through freedom from superstitions. Superstitious people defend their own ignorance and bondage, enslaving others in the process. Freedom is not an illusion, a rumor. Believe in freedom as the higher goal for which we fight.

Defending freedom in an oppressed and classed society that has conflicting interests is not easy. In such a society each person champions what they imagine freedom to be, but few are those who seek the mysteries of freedom from the position of freedom.

13 points on Shamlou's ideas about art and society:

1. It is important to distinguish between political literature and socially engaged literature. Social Realism was the aesthetic doctrine of the Communist Party, but neither Shamlou nor other writers worldwide, such as Mario Vargas Llosa, could get behind *political* literature, which espoused literature as propaganda, a vehicle for disseminating political ideas to the proletariat. For example, though many of Shamlou's socially themed poems were written while he was imprisoned, he did not consider any of them political poems, per se. To Shamlou, politics was such a dirty game that the mere hint of it soiled the very hem of the skirt of poetry.

2. Shamlou believed that the masses could not directly connect with the work of an innovator, whose primary job it was to incite innovation. An intermediary was needed to make the connection. Yet these works, which would not pander to the masses, were not to be confused with "bourgeois art." Therefore, there was no "people's art" in the literal sense of the word.

3. Shamlou's critics attacked some of his work for being personal and not socially minded, and others for being deeply rooted in the events of his time, incapable of passing the test of time. But rather than succumb to the division of his works into eras, or react to such assessments, or try to please the critics, Shamlou remained unfazed. His intention was never to use poetry as a means with which to fit himself into society. He was not running a poetry factory, he said, to conduct market research on what kind of poetry people wanted so as to produce that marketable product.

4. Shamlou traced the seeds of the criticism that his work was not socially engaged to the 1950s and 1960s when junior members of the Communist Party, believing themselves proficient in cultural theory, yet whose knowledge, he said, did not equip them to distinguish between a mule and an ass, spouted off the idea that art should be *for* and understandable *by* the masses. Their ideas were directly lifted from the *Zhdanov Doctrine*, formulated by Stalin and his cultural agent, Zhdanov, and revered as scripture. The doctrine reduced all of culture to a sort of chart, wherein a given symbol corresponded to a simple moral value.

5. The masses were stratified, not monolithic. There were the illiterate, the semi-literate, the absolutely uninspired, the somewhat inspired, the inspired illiterate, the uninspired semi-literate and so on. Which "mass art" was to appeal to which of these substrata? What of high art, in the works of, for example, Tchaikovsky, Mussorgsky, and Glinka, upholders of the Russian musical heritage? (Shamlou cleverly mentioned Russian composers so that "friends" in the Communist Party could not dismiss his point for citing artists who had "betrayed" the proletariat.) Those composers channeled Russian national and folk themes in their compositions, themes that the masses, such as the semi-literate lumberjack in remote forests of Siberia, hummed and connected with as the very raw material of his soul. Shamlou questioned whether those composers' innovative works were mass or high art in the eyes of Communist ideologues.

6. Shamlou said that literature is produced by singular literary workers from their own experiences. No clear path could be drawn for literature. Necessity is the mother of invention—what arrives at a point of urgency is a done deal. It can neither be rushed nor impeded.

7. This is a reminder of T.S. Eliot's essay, "Tradition and the Individual Talent," in which Eliot points out that scoffing at the notion of "tradition" is a failure to recognize that what is known and disparaged as "tradition" at any given time was a leap of innovation in its time, once a transgression that was likely resisted, mocked, and written off. So to

dismiss it as passé or old-fashioned is paradoxical in some way, in that it subsumes innovation, the future.

8. Shamlou said that his poetry stemmed from his own pain. How honest would his poetry be if it pretended to be cried out from other people's pain? Yet, he said, *If my pain were common, then I have at once cried our common pain.* Hence the lines, *I am common pain/cry me out!* (from Shamlou's poem, *"Collective Love"*).

9. The irony is in that "commercial art," popular amongst the masses, and devoid of any meaning, is in fact the enemy of a people's culture, further distancing them from their freedom, enslaving them instead. In contrast, there is art that is not popular, but whose content is deeply pro-proletariat. Art that contains slogans for the masses should really count as "political activity," not "cultural activity," and the basis of its measure should be "historical value" not "cultural value."

10. For the innovations of a lasting work of art to reach all strata of society, other artists with access to both the innovators' visions and the masses were needed to act as intermediaries, to transmute the art for them. An example of such an intermediary was the Iranian poet, journalist, and leftist activist Khosrow Golesorkhi, executed by the Shah's regime and the dedicatee of Shamlou's poem, *"Rupture."* [5]

11. Shamlou considered the colloquial language he had been exposed to in his early years to be much richer and more expressive than the official language. He began to fuse high and low language together to create a new, multidimensional one. To him, the writer who embodied his or her time must make these two poles speak with each other. He struck a fine balance in his straddling of both high and low cultures. The Iranian poet and critic Mohammad Reza Shafiei Kadkani believed that even if Shamlou's language spanned the vernacular registers of the street to the higher, more erudite ones, Shamlou managed to never write a common poem in his long career.

12. In Moslem Mansouri's documentary, *The Final Word*—a different cut of which is presented as *Master Poet of Liberty*, an apt title for the poet of the people's heart—Shamlou said that commitment was not implicit in the nature of art itself. It is the artist who has to be committed, bear witness to history. If artists do not understand the pain of humanity, they cannot be considered intellectuals—they are merely thieves with a torch.

13. Shamlou thought that many conflated the notion of social commitment to make art for the people with an imaginary debt that the artist owed to society.

As a translator, Shamlou brought dozens of international works into Persian. In this way, he had at his disposal several literary traditions, and aesthetic and poetic movements, a broad sampling of world literatures to draw from in concocting a unique recipe that fomented his cultural revolution. What made Shamlou the avant-garde poet of his time, beyond his unparalleled mastery of the Persian language and literary history, was his power of synthesizing through the filter of his own imagination and creativity all of the literatures from which he drew.

Even if he himself did not have direct access to most of the languages from which he translated, collaborating from trots—literal translations of foreign texts—provided by language intermediaries, the practice of translating not only informed Shamlou's own work, but it put him in direct conversation with a global knowledge base. Translation, a tool with which he bridged the world to his own work, bled into his own poems, a grafting of aesthetic innovations of other literatures to imagery from classical Persian literature to new subjects and languages, creating a third language.

Translating gave Shamlou the opportunity to deploy and experiment with the vernacular: street language in Langston Hughes' work and in

Mikhail Sholokhov's *And Quiet Flows the Don*, and everyday language in the works of Lorca and Margot Bickel, to name a few.

Some of Shamlou's translations were twice removed from their original sources. Shamlou's knowledge of the Soviet poet Vladimir Mayakovsky's work, for example, which informed his poem, *"The Final Word,"* came from French translations of the Russian originals. He translated ideas, images, prosody, music, language, tone, techniques, patterns. His creative renderings—and occasional errors—all played an integral part in the fresh air that he breathed into Persian poetics, shaping the disruptions he made. In many ways, Shamlou's importing of international literatures and ideas into his native one was equally, if not more, disruptive as Ezra Pound's, whose translations and introductions of Chinese and Japanese poetry into English changed the course of American poetics, still reverberating in the poetic practice one century later.

In importing and remixing ideas, Shamlou also drew from a wide swath of sources beyond the page: the protest music of the executed Chilean artist, activist, and songwriter Victor Jara, the Greek composer Mikis Theodorakis' rendering of Neruda's homage to his continent, *Canto General*, classical music, and films are a few of the works I remember being introduced to personally.

Shamlou not only wrote and adapted a number of seminal works for children, including the iconic works, *Pariyah* (*The Fairies*) and *Dokhtaraye Naneh Darya* (*The Daughters of Mother Sea*), in that familiar yet new language that he created at the crossroads of the high and low, he also translated Antoine de Saint-Exupéry's *The Little Prince*. For some time, he was considering my little brother, whose voice had not yet turned, as the little prince for the dramatic recording of the work he was preparing.

In a 1972 article in *Keyhan-e Sal* magazine, Shamlou expressed his dissatisfaction with existing Persian translations of the novels *Virgin Soil*

Upturned and Sholokhov's *And Quiet Flows the Don*, the latter of which Shamlou later translated, satisfying the poet's love for the novel and the epic. Shamlou posed the question as to whether social commitment alone sufficed for literary workers, and whether that commitment could override a broader commitment to literature and language. He questioned whether a subpar translation—be it through sheer neglect, the absence of knowledge, or linguistic weakness—was excusable if the literary worker creating it was socially committed.

On July 30, 2010, on the occasion of the tenth anniversary of the poet's passing, Faraj Sarkoohi writes in a BBC Persian online article that Shamlou rejected the approach of word by word, phrase by phrase, and in the case of poetry, verse by verse translation, arguing that the translation of poetry, as opposed to prose, hinged on the strength of the internal music and language of the rendition. The only option was the re-recitation of a poem in the target language. Poetry was to be translated in the obliteration and re-creation anew in language.

While Shamlou was inventive and literary in his translation output, he was neither always accurate—looking up terms in reference books and sometimes translating word by word—nor was he, by his own admission, always faithful, believing instead that the translator had to edit in the interest of the final work and its audience, lest the work be suspended in some linguistic and cultural limbo. In the documentary *The Final Word,* Shamlou mentioned his intervening in the translation of a short story by Kafka, whose language he found complex and in need of some kneading into Persian. Essentially, in his practice, Shamlou broadened the notion of "faithful" in translation, prioritizing artfulness and accessibility in the new language over a strict adherence to words in the original.

But Shamlou also thought that translation could at most transmit meaning, images, ideas, imaginary figments, that language and the internal music of a poem was lost in translation. In other words, what was lost in the translation of poetry was poetry. Did he think this applied to himself as a poet or as a translator, or both? These comments coming from a writer who translated a vast body of international literature reveal Shamlou's quite complex relationship with translation.

Shamlou was arrested and held as a political prisoner just after the 1953 coup d'état orchestrated by the United Kingdom under the name "Operation Boot" and the United States under the name "Operation Ajax." Political prisons were packed with people from all strata of society in close quarters. University professors, farmers, merchants, and laborers were eating together, commiserating, exchanging ideas. Away from home, desperate to forget their surroundings, they came together, told stories, recited poetry, hummed songs together. Early among these songs was a lullaby Shamlou composed, *"Laalaa'i,"* a folkloric song gathered and edited by him, a practice he would continue to masterful levels for the rest of his life. This poem of resistance circulated, filled prisoners up with hope and the zeal to fight.

Laa laai laai lai laai lai, little rosebud
your daddy's gone, my heart is blood
Laa laai laai, your daddy's not coming home tonight
maybe they've taken your daddy, laa laai laai
Laa laai laai lai laai lai, little iron bud
the enemy killed your daddy
Laa laai laai, this is the enemy's mark
hands soaked with blood, laa laai laai
sleep peacefully in your cradle tonight, laa laai laai
like fire in ashes, laa laai laai
tomorrow you'll ignite
avenging daddy's blood, laa laai laai...

In his estimation of his own work, Shamlou's first serious volume of poetry was *Fresh Air* (1956), the publication of which was an *event* in Iranian poetics, largely inspired by Paul Éluard's poem, *"Air Vif,"* from his 1951 volume, *Le Phénix,* which Shamlou translated and published under the title *"Fresh Air"* in 1955:

I looked before me
I saw you in the crowd
I saw you among the wheat
I saw you under a tree

At the end of my journeys
In the depths of my torment
At the corner of every smile
Emerging from water and fire

I saw you summer and winter
I saw you throughout my house
I saw you in my arms
I saw you in my dreams
I will never leave you.

Shamlou's poem, *"Collective Love,"* from his volume, *Fresh Air,* is especially reminiscent of Éluard's *"Air Vif."*

In 1954, when Shamlou was making his young mark on poetry and struggling to break with tradition, he composed one of his most well-known poems, *"Poetry That is Life,"* while imprisoned, witnessing poets and activists tortured and executed. The long poem is considered his version of Archibald MacLeish's poem, "Ars Poetica," a poem about what a poem should be, which ends with, "A poem should not mean/But be."

Shamlou echoes this sentiment in *"Poetry That is Life."* In the poem, a poet breaks out into the streets declaring to "everyman" that his poetry is for and about *them,* not the irrelevant subjects of the past.

The subject matter of poetry
from past poets was not life.

...

The subject of poetry
today
is a different matter...

Today
poetry
is the weapon of the masses
because poets are themselves
one branch from the forest of the masses,
not jasmines and hyacinths from so-and-so's greenhouse.

Shamlou's call to arms served as a manifesto of the new emancipatory poetics in which, following the prescription of his mentor, Nima, a poet must embody the essence of his or her time through an expression that is stripped of pretenses and decorative language. And this would be the measure of the best poets across time. Because life came first.

3. AIDA:
MUSE, WIFE, ASSISTANT, STEWARD

BY 1962, AFTER A SECOND DIVORCE and fatherhood duties dodged, Shamlou has moved to his mother's house to start over yet again.

Next door, from the upstairs bedroom window, a young woman spies on the man with the curly head of hair scribbling in the front yard. Her name would become Aida Shamlou, née Rita Athans Sarkisian on November 15, 1939, in Tehran into an Armenian-Iranian family.

Mrs. Shamlou recounts to me by phone: *Ahmad would stand by the lawn in the yard and sometimes I would stand on our balcony. We communicated through music, each playing a record on the gramophone in response to the other. Once he walked up to the balcony and asked whether my name was Aida, but I remained coy. Finally, one day I found Shamlou holding up to me on my balcony a placard with his phone number written on it. I blushed. We didn't have a telephone, so I had to walk to the newly opened supermarket—the first one in Iran, I might add—where there was a public telephone. Our first conversation was fireworks. He talked about everything. I couldn't believe it. He would fetch me after class at the college for secretaries and walk me home. We sat on park benches and he would talk for hours. I thought, who is this man?*

She continues: *One day at dusk, there was a strange summer rainstorm. The next day I went to their house, but Ahmad wasn't there, so I waited for him on his bed, with my back leaning against the wall. All of a sudden I turned around and saw a poem called* "Aida in the Mirror," *written in pencil on the wall, dated the night before. I was stunned. Just then, Shamlou walked in and saw me reading it. He told me to read it out loud. He always asked me to read his poems aloud. He said matter of factly that the poem had woken him up in the middle of the night begging to be written, but he couldn't find paper, so he wrote it on the wall. The poem was published without a single edit. For Shamlou, poetry bubbled from the fountain within. The first steps taken were from a sort of madness. His poems came through a trance.*

I could never access that side of him, she said. *I was young, but I knew I never wanted to be with anyone else. I gave him my life, to help him soar from the muddy swamps. I couldn't watch his greatness go to waste. When we had money, we lived. When we didn't, we had each other. He was an endless universe. I was by his side for forty years. What else could anyone want? My epic hero, my majestic man!*

For them, everything started with a first glance. Love first, then familiarity.

You know the rest: Wife Eternal—and still.

Aida treated Shamlou as her personal responsibility. It was improbable for any other woman to serve Shamlou in this way. Before Aida, Shamlou had not experienced *woman*. And there were many in Shamlou's life, but none who could give him the peace and space he needed, as both Aida and Shamlou concur in *The Final Word*. If previous encounters had been inspiring, he would have preserved those relationships, he said.

Shamlou wondered what role love played in the life of writers who did not write of their lovers and beloveds. To Aida, the poems that Shamlou recited *for* her, the personal poems, were his most socially conscious ones, and the social poems were really about their lives.

In Aida, Shamlou found not only a woman with whom he had instant chemistry, but also a muse of sorts who appeared just at the right moment when Shamlou had abandoned attempts at a conventional life, rejecting the limitations that the values of a middle-class life would impose on him. Aida instantly took it upon herself to create the conducive environment in which Ahmad would become Shamlou. She volunteered to become engulfed by Shamlou's life. They both imbued the elusive moment of their meeting with mythical symbolism, a pivotal union.

But muse would not encompass the totality of Aida's role. She was assistant, lifelong devotee, and steward. Aida is widely credited with an honorary role in the birth of Modern Poetry in Iran for the care she took of Shamlou, launching a new phase in his life, and for the work she did alongside, and after him, supervising the ongoing work of posthumous publications and so much more, though she would reject any such credit. Shamlou's inscription in one of his books, summarized here, attests to her involvement from the very beginning:

Dearest one, this is not like any other book whose first copy I bring home to dedicate to you and watch the glee of another one of my successes in the electricity of your eyes. It is not only the product of the love you give me, the loving and secure setting you provide me, my work, and my life. It is also the result of your invaluable collaborations. One day you might pick it up and remember the spring nights of our tenth year, the nights when you heard my voice narrating and wrote the translations down, when we lost ourselves in these words. The white pages will reflect on your face, and you will be beautiful as ever...

Shamlou's poetic expressions of ideals circled around a collective humanism, not injustices specific to women. When Aida was muse in Shamlou's love poetry, he wrote both in her name, as well as inspired by her. He portrayed Aida as the idealized Woman, the fantasy female who offered pure love and onto whom Shamlou's yearnings for both a harmonious humanity and an intimate refuge could be projected. In effect, Shamlou was Pygmalion, transforming Aida through the force of his poetry into the figure of Love, an external reality of an ideal. And who better than the graceful, well-spoken, restrained, faithful, soft, and beautiful Aida, the perfect lady of the poetic imagination.

Aida and Shamlou, steadfast in their life-transforming love, believed that only love could save humans. Nothing could come forth without a heart filled with love.

If only all artists had their own Aida.

Aida, whom I called *Khaleh* or Auntie Aida, was a tall, slim, elegant woman with long, straight hair and the impossibly high cheekbones of a screen siren. I can scarcely believe that she is an old woman now, face shrunken, eyes narrowed and watery, hair unkempt and grey. I can only see this through a rare and somewhat recent photo of her on the internet, wrapped in a scarf and *manto* (a long body coat), date unknown but unmistakably since Shamlou's death in 2000, evident by the all black all the time. She will be more withered now in real life, her indifference about her appearance betraying her monastic abandon to him, the man of her myths, her legend. I don't remember much about her. I cannot remember whether she spent her time in the divided company of women in the kitchen or men being waited on in the living room. Maybe she oscillated between the two realms, not being any old housewife, yet only the bride and extension of a great man. What was in the living room? Men taking space, their voices carrying, their hands extended toward the center of the coffee table, reaching for *ajeel*, trail mix, snapping open sunflower and watermelon seeds between their teeth and popping pistachios and hazelnuts into their mouths between expletives and opinions, sweetening the nuts with golden or green raisins. Their hands reaching for tiny pickles to dip in the yogurt, chasers for the homemade hard liquor or the black-market beer. Pabst Blue Ribbon, my first beer.

Tehran, Iran, 1983 — Windows are lit up for the evening, bulbs glinting. Outside a clear sky. Imagine Van Gogh's 1888 painting, *Café Terrace at Night*.

Anxious, I save it until dinner is over. After I play the ethereal first movement of the *Moonlight Sonata*—all I ever learned of that piece—in a private piano recital for the poet and his wife, and my parents, who are entertaining them on our veranda, I dutifully walk outside, a young lady awkwardly taking her bows in the night.

The poet says:

That was so beautiful. I see that you played all the notes "forte" so that I could hear them from here.

I had tutoring in any subject I desired. Madame Markarian was only one sentinel in the army of my educators. I also went to drawing and painting classes with my mother, who still paints.

It seems miraculous that a few of my early canvases made it through the ordeal of escaping one country for another, and even stopping at a third in the middle to get papers in order, as we did. One particular time capsule that survived was an early 8x10 plein-air painting of an open field, golden stalks swaying against the backdrop of a country home, rows of trees, and a vast horizontal sky. Spiked dollops of oil paint raised an eighth of an inch from the surface to show texture. And I cannot believe that I gradually discarded them over the years as I moved from one U.S. city to another.

My English tutor, the good-natured and dashing, British-educated Indian, Mr. Rajen or Mr. Rajan, I can't be sure of the spelling now—whom we called *Mester Rajen*—popped sugar cubes into the well of his mouth from the silver tray of afternoon *chai* my mother would serve during our weekly sessions at my large desk in my blue bedroom, that temple of wonders, my back to the same window of the snowfall spell. He only inhaled the tea as a gesture of afterthought, a show of gratitude for my mother's trouble, or perhaps to wash down those six sugar cubes he crunched one after the other between his yellowish piano-key teeth, which I had the chance to view often, bedazzling his winsome smile, a sweeping curve like the coliseum. I owe my English to him. And the taste of curry. And the very first mention of Elvis Presley by his teenage daughter who, possessed by a full-scale crush, was shocked at my ignorance of the superstar, her large recriminating eyes on an embarrassed schoolgirl across the table at one of Tehran's posh Indian restaurants where my family once treated Mr. Rajen's to a formal Friday luncheon—the only time I ever met his family, all of them in traditional dress. I had never even imagined him with one before.

It is perhaps pharmacists who spread rumors about physicians having chicken scratch for handwriting. I would, too, if I were a pharmacist. To have to correctly decipher hastily scribbled prescriptions for the despondent sick standing before you dispatched by invisible physicians practicing their lofty art in the upper floors. But my father's handwriting was and remains measured, legible, noble even. He used to make me tapes, spending blissful hours in his music room transferring music from his records, meticulously labeling the cassettes and inserts. One of the tapes that traveled with me to this continent was a recording of Beethoven's Piano Concerto no. 4—I cannot recall which version. I played it hundreds of times throughout the 1980s in my car, at home, until I foolishly loaned it to some trusted friend as my favorite version of my favorite piece. I never got it back. But even if I had, I am not sure the pianist, conductor, and orchestra were marked on the cassette. So while I searched for years to come for that rendition at record stores—because at that time, I still remembered every nuance of that particular recording— I never recovered it, to this day unsure whose version I loved, against which every other version was compared, and rejected. Our measure of future versions is firmly based on the very first version we hear, repeat, and internalize. Now, the nuances are all but forgotten, only major markers about the piece remain, a *feeling* about that second movement, perhaps my favorite second movement of any piano concerto.

The first color I associated with the poet was white. Later, it became red. But for many years, it was pure white in our living room.

Ribbons of smoke coiled up from a head of wild, white curls. Beethoven hair. White cigarettes nestled between his beefy fingers held at his full lips that opened in the shape of a dolphin's mouth.

Years later, I saw a three-quarter profile photo of him in a red shirt, and his color turned to red. Red for risk. Red for sacrifice. Red for the people.

Red for wound.

While I writhe from periodic spasms
waves rise and swell in me.
An awareness gathers inside
stirs the infinite in
the grains that make me.

The poet, lover of the poor and tyrannized, warriors
appears giant-like in my home.
He leads me wild dances to
Chopin,
      Rachmaninov,
         Beethoven,
            Ravel,
              Lalo,
                Tchaikovsky,
                   Yupanqui.

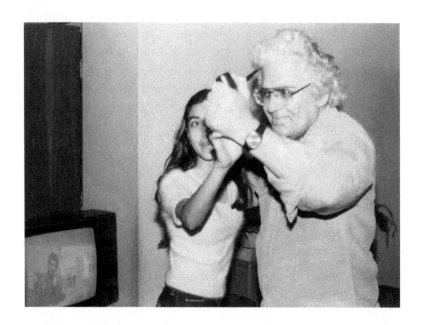

On the night this photo was taken, Chopin waltzes were played at our home. I was twelve or thirteen wearing a thick, mint-green angora sweater handed down from my mother that was a size nothing. And not terribly stretchy by virtue of its thickness. It would be too itchy for me now. But my tolerance was high then. I was wearing it with brand new, bone-tight jeans. I was tall for my age, slender, upright. I don't know whether the waltz stirred me to my feet (that would not have been normally encouraged), which got Shamlou to spring up and grab me in a dance, or whether the music moved him to grab me. I certainly had never waltzed. I think it was my mother who snapped the photo, the only time she would have been exhilarated at the sight of me dancing, since she had deemed me a not-so-good dancer, or dancing not so discreet, though I was always dancing. And still am. The television was airing some forced confession or propaganda charade or war lie. We must have spun in circles. Or he may have just done a pendulum side-to-side step, pipe in hand.

Shamlou would autograph this image for me years later.

Tehran, Iran, 1983 — A father and daughter standing at the tall French window in their new living room, the rich afternoon light surging obliquely through the glass. A frozen image. We see their backs, as if a Magritte painting. My father on the right, and I, his teenage daughter, on the left, watching the jolly neighbor's wife across the street jesting about in her muumuu.

My father asks,

Would you rather be dim and happy or knowing and suffer?

The temptation to eat from the Tree
of the Knowledge of Good and Evil.

5. SHAMLOU

SHAMLOU HAD THE UTMOST FAITH in the richness of the Persian language and its expressive abilities. Reciting poetry in such an imagistic language, he said, was his pleasure. If each generation's responsibility is to create a new language, a tool that captures and expresses the new needs and experiences of that generation, then Shamlou not only accomplished this for his own, but his shadow was so imposing that the generation following him was challenged in extricating itself from it.

He worried that his influence might have cost a generation valuable time. Daily life was enough of a drain on artists' time—not on the merchants'—and he lamented that censorship had cost Iran's thinkers much precious time.

Versed literature was not necessarily poetry to Shamlou. To him, the greatest damage to language was the inability of poets to innovate imaginatively in language, perhaps from a fundamental ignorance of it. Shamlou worried that the absence of meter in his poetry had misled the newer generations to bypass the crucial step of learning craft, as he had done before breaking the rules, instead expressing themselves in unmetered language not built upon the foundations of language.

Shamlou had embarked on designing a new mosaic from old tiles. His poetry at once elevated and popularized poetry.

Shamlou wrote that after a centuries-long period of dormancy, Iranian poetry had undergone an awakening, shining in the landscape of world literature on its own merits, owing its powers to ideas synthesized from both international and domestic aesthetic and intellectual movements.

And although Shamlou's first exposure to modern poetry came through Western poetry, he resisted the charge of Westernization or "Westoxification" (as coined by the Iranian writer Jalal Al-Ahmad).

He poignantly remarked that unless Iranians count the adoption of various industries including textiles, oil refineries, airplanes, automobiles, and elevators as a Westernized practice, unless they limit their weaponry to swords and spears or limit medicine to the tinctures and distillates of yesteryear, they were, in fact, participating in a global trade of cultural collateral in the same way that science and industry were traded. Humanity progresses in sync, he said. Anything short of that would be severing Iranian society from the whole of humanity, a self-sanctioning.

And at the same time, Shamlou resisted being "othered" by the West. In May 1976, Shamlou delivered a speech at the joint PEN American Center and Princeton University event on the subject of "Contemporary Literature in the Middle East":

In my country, a Muslim-majority country, the Koran is considered a miracle. This is easy to say, but beyond the obvious lies something astonishing.

In my country, there are many figures belonging to the rank of miracle-makers. Those known in the West are the prophet Mani and his miracle, the holy Book of Arjang, as well as Rumi, whose status as a prophet is certifiable. Hafez, the fourteenth century poet of a divan of ghazals, is also known here in the West. In my country, he is known as "lisan al-ghayb," meaning he who speaks of mysteries, which in my opinion means more than a prophet, it's really the speaker of a "language of god." So in my country, the Koran and the Divan are of the same stature.

I know I am a poet saying such things about poets, but please disregard that in favor of the truth. In my country, people deem poets as prophets onto whom they bestow enviable love. If a poet has passed their ruthless judgment and been accepted as a poet, and if the poet is not a follower of common traditions, then that poet is elevated to the status of martyr. In Iran, my country, a poetry reading is nothing short of an EVENT. The young generation still remembers the poetry festival that Khoosheh *journal co-organized when I was its editor-in-chief as an unforgettable memory. During the festival week, 2,000–3,000 young people gathered at the civil servant's garden from 6 p.m. to midnight to hear dozens of poets who had paid their own way to Tehran from all corners of Iran. So I don't see any reason to waste your precious time here to tell you how I see poetry. From a craft standpoint, it is the artistry of language, or something like that. Either way, I am not a poetry critic. I live in a terrible world, worse than terrible—looking at the world with two open eyes, rage and desolation eat me alive, and I, with thirty-two teeth, my own liver. The people of my country expect miracles of their prophets. And let me tell you with deep pride—for even if you speak different languages, you still have the same heart—that your contemporary poets in Iran have accomplished, without an ounce of pride and self-promotion, such miracles, the products of their creativity and innovations such that rival the linguistic prowess of Ferdowsi and Hafez.*

So let me summarize: Poetry is whatever it is. Contemporary poets in Iran have accomplished the task of bearing noble witness to their times.

The Shamlous visited us first at the small apartment in the complex of tall, sooty buildings whose main attraction to us kids was what seemed like an Olympic-sized swimming pool next to a large and shallow kids' pool, and later at the white-colored house my parents built, their dream home we abandoned only two years later to emigrate in 1984. The first apartment was walking distance to my father's clinic, a walk my mother and I made many times through sleepy side streets either to meet my father, which mostly turned into a fun eye doctor's appointment for me as I explored every inch of what seemed like a vast room, with a desk area, an eye exam area, and an adjoining room for contact lens fittings, or for one of us to be examined for some illness by a colleague on a different floor, as I was an often-sick child, perhaps a byproduct of ultra-clean mothering and the frequent and abundant access to antibiotics at any sign of a cold, or some such reason. We could see the crosses on the steeples of the Armenian church, Saint Sarkis, right at the center of Tehran. The second home was the white, Greco-Roman-style one-story house my parents built on the parcel of land they had purchased at a new development on the western outskirts of Tehran, the construction of which was the subject of endless nihilistic speculation as to whether their nest egg should be spent on a property in a country whose present was one unexpected and shocking charade after another, and whose future was uncertain, if not outright bleak.

We also visited the Shamlous' apartment in Tehran. It was here that I first encountered artichokes, in the form of hearts brined in vinegar. The precious few of them served in a little bowl seemed so exotic and Western, as if they were not to be eaten, as if they must have cost a hefty sum on the black market that gave my family access to Corn Flakes, peanut butter, and other Western foods. But artichokes I had never seen. I chalked up the canned hearts to Aida's Christian Armenian background. But I wonder now whether it had more to do with exposure through their travels abroad, which somehow my own travels had not furnished me with.

On the tour of the apartment, we were shown Shamlou's office, his writing sanctuary, with a small desk, and small pieces of paper, called *fiche*, with little notes. Now I know those were entries for the *Book of the Alley*, the living compendium of folklore Shamlou had begun gathering early on in his life—but had abandoned many times after the manuscripts were confiscated in raids, burned, lost—which went through fits and starts before he resumed gathering for the third time in 1965.

On one occasion, Shamlou played Tchaikovsky's 1812 Overture, a piece depicting and commemorating Russia's defense of its motherland against Napoleon's invasion in 1812. The piece ends with five explosive cannon shots to counter a fragment of "La Marseillaise," the French national anthem, and climaxes in a volley of thundering with eleven more precisely scored shots, chimes, and brass fanfare such that it is a common accompaniment to fireworks displays.

In the middle of the final fanfare, their intercom rang. Shamlou answered. On the other end was a frantic neighbor pleading that they stop the music. It was too close to the sound of bombs. And Tehran had been bombed during the Iran-Iraq war. On a few occasions, my family and other residents of our apartment complex had taken shelter in the basement of the tall apartment buildings, huddling together and shuffling around the damp and dingy corridors candle in hand. Maybe we all made light of the frantic neighbor, maybe it was yet another reminder of the reality of uncertain times.

While Shamlou reworked his understanding of poetry as a weapon in the struggle for liberation, yet distinguish it as art rather than active participation in the struggle, the guerrilla poets of the 1970s, Sa'id Soltanpour and Saeed Yousef prominent among them, went in the opposite direction, arguing that poets could and must serve as combatants. The execution of poet and leftist organizer Khosrow Golesorkhi in February 1974 provided the younger generation of committed poets with their own native archetype of the poet-activist-martyr, an avatar of the idea that poets, if not also their poems, could participate in the struggle.

Shamlou's 1974 book of poems, *Abraham in Flames*, contains twenty-one poems written from 1970–1973, an ode to freedom fighters and risk-takers, a few of the poems dedicated to specific people who were executed by the Shah's regime for their resistance. It is a dark book about standing up to oppressors, evoking images of falling to bloody deaths in public squares, braving trials by fire, the intermingling of earth and blood, and fields of flowers blooming from bloodshed.

The title poem, *"Abraham in Flames,"* invokes the young Biblical Abraham who came from a family of idol sellers, but who believed in the one true God. Abraham was condemned to burn at the stake by Nimrod, the king of Babylon. The largest fire the world had ever seen was lit, flames so high that birds would not fly over it for fear of burning. Just as Abraham was being thrown in, the archangel Gabriel appeared and asked if Abraham wished for anything.

Abraham asked for nothing, relinquishing flesh to fire, which burned only his chains, Abraham emerging from it as if from a garden, peaceful, face illuminated.

Shamlou admittedly succumbed to a sort of pessimism around this time. He lost faith, everything seeming like a silly game. Many of his contemporaries suffered similarly, some died, and others changed. He became a shell of a man. He felt the only way he could save himself, his conscience, and be true to himself, was suicide. It was Aida who turned things around, Aida, his embodiment of beauty in the world, restoring his faith in purity and humanity. In a way, this ruin was the beginning of a new discovery.

In a 2015 interview with *Madomeh* online journal, Aida reminisced:

In 1974, after the executions of Khosrow Golesorkhi and others, and then the arrest of Gholam-Hossein Saedi, the atmosphere became even more oppressive. Shamlou was destroyed, restless, unable to concentrate. Sometimes he even wept. But the threat of censorship and the possibility of not being published never shook his creativity, the actual creation of the work, the endless hours at his desk. Agitated, yes, but admittedly, "thick-skinned and brazen," there would be no stopping Shamlou.

In 1975 when Shamlou's book of poems, *Dagger in the Tray*, was slated to be published, he was summoned by the Savak (the Shah-era secret state organization of intelligence and security in Iran that determined what was permitted and what was not). Literature was routinely and expectedly monitored. In turn, adapting to the censorship, writers would invent new codes. "Wheat" as metaphor for X, "green" for Y, "red" for Z. When those systems were decoded, new ones were invented, and so on. The censor asked Shamlou to save everyone time and just point to the sections in his work that were critical of the regime. Shamlou's response:

That is your job, mine is to write.

Of censors, Shamlou said: *The censor is in terror of himself, fears the revelation of truth, for he himself is nothing more than deceit. Censorship is the definitive block against the influx of constructive ideas, what every totalitarian regime is in terror of.*

The intimidation and repression was so stifling in those days that even close friends were suspicious of each other. Shamlou decided to leave the country. Aida knew just what could ground him. Shamlou had dreamt of someday running his own publishing house to print books banned in Iran to send back home. He believed deeply in the power of children's books. They left for the United States and settled in New Brunswick, New Jersey, with the intention of starting a journal and publishing activities under the impression of secured financial support.

While abroad, Shamlou insisted that correspondence to and from Iran not bear their names so as to keep secret his plans to publish a political journal. He wanted Aida to be referred to by her given name, Rita. There were delays in receiving the newspaper, *Keyhan*, from Iran, as they were forwarded with Shamlou's actual name on the envelope. Shamlou was despondent in the absence of news on the status of his works.

Laying the groundwork for his journal, he picked the name *"Cheragh,"* meaning light or torch. He dove in, had a logo designed in calligraphy, but collaborations and support did not proceed in the U.S. They left for England on an invitation from the publisher of *Iranshahr* weekly journal to assume the role of editor-in-chief. There were disagreements, and Shamlou resigned on January 19, 1979, after the thirteenth issue, and returned to Iran on March 3, 1979, only weeks after the revolution was declared "victorious."

Shamlou was published by both large publishers and small, independent presses that he championed. He experienced his fair share of entanglements with the various presses, not the least of which were delays in publishing, grey areas in royalties, and other complications from the banning of his books. In the winter of 1983, for example, two months after the third book of the letter "A" of the *Book of the Alley* was published, it was banned, and copies of the volume were subsequently stored in a warehouse for nine years. Certainly, this would raise issues related to storage fees for those many years. Aida Shamlou wrote that they are still not clear on how many copies and editions of Shamlou's *Divan of Hafez* were published, since each new printing perpetually hovers around the seventh or eighth edition.

Shamlou was never for sale: *Artists are always in power, not with the powers that be. Let those who want to be with power hang themselves with the elastic band of whichever president's underwear. Their being alive or dead makes no difference to me.*

In September 1977, the late Dr. Ehsan Yarshater, founder of the Encyclopedia Iranica project, invited Shamlou to edit his encyclopedia at Columbia University, offering him a salary and two dedicated assistants. Shamlou accepted the invitation. However, immediately after, an article was published in Iran announcing this news, but also announcing a million-dollar gift to Columbia University by the Empress Farah Pahlavi Foundation for the Advancement of Persian Culture and Languages. On November 2, rejecting any connection with the gift and its source, Shamlou returned his first payment and released himself from the offer.

Shamlou embodied his time, fought against injustice in the brutal face of history. Grief stewed in him to find expression. Beyond declamations and outrage and ideological differences was Shamlou, the solitary poet-seer, poet-healer, witness for the voiceless, with a charge to exorcise his tortured existence, "to forge the uncreated conscience of [his] race…" (James Joyce, *A Portrait of the Artist as a Young Man*).

6. ME

MY MOTHER BEGAN TO PLAY THE PIANO in her thirties. Surrounded by music and greatness, she longed for more than three hot meals a day and the tyranny of laundry and homework and a claustrophobic life caring about what everyone else thought. She was child-like at the piano, sturdy, elegant hands, onion-skin nail polish, occasionally, very occasionally, red. Whispering, *do, mi, sol, do*.

Sometimes at twilight, my mother's heart tightened. Dusk was the hour of the unrealized.

Scales after scales. Painstaking scales between immaculate hospitality, beef stroganoff, lamb rice, yogurt dip for the illegal sour cherry *vishnovka* brewed I don't know where in that small apartment from my surgeon father's supply of alcohol. Alcoholic beverages were banned after the revolution, yet present at some gatherings. No, no one went blind from drinking medicinal alcohol. I watched on the sidelines as my mother and other women carried on the theater of domesticity. It was at one of these gatherings that I got my first taste of beer and cigarettes from guests who crowded me in the cubby of the kitchen where the washer and dryer were nestled, one jovially handing me a Pabst Blue Ribbon and the other slipping me a lit Winston cigarette, laughing as I cringed from the bitter effervescence and coughed from the inhalation as my parents were up in arms.

My mother played more scales. To begin like this at the beginning, to always be the newest beginner. I know something of this courage.

I first heard Ravel's *Bolero* with Shamlou and my father, the three of us standing and staring at the gramophone as if it were a stage at a concert hall. I felt a connection between the crescendo in *Bolero* and the soaring buildup in a scene of one of the regime's propaganda films pushing the agenda of Islam. The scene was a long shot of a caravan of the prophet

Mohammad's followers traversing a desert landscape against a dramatic sky. Perhaps it was the exodus from Mecca to Medina. The music evoked momentousness, a climax. Feeling the connection, I remarked, *Amoo*—meaning uncle, how male family friends are addressed in Iran—*Shamlou, this is like that scene in the Mohammad film when they are crossing a desert.* He laughed, missing the point I intended to make, admittedly not made well, and said, *Except that those people were going*—and then he showed a downward gesture with his arm—*the opposite way.* I was deeply embarrassed at not having posed the observation more specifically. What if he thought I had newfound religious zeal?! I might have spoken up to clarify that I was referring to similarity in musical *buildup.* But alas, I did not. I had not yet learned how to be laser sharp with language, to make space for myself when my first try did not resonate. So many dimensions budding in me at that time that I was not communicating. The world was opening itself to me in continuous waves.

I was fortunate. I had sensitive, passionate parents who listened and heard and felt every wave and nuance and turn. I learned early to hear, watching my parents respond to the hush at the stillness and pause of the Beethoven second movement, the heroic journey of the piano toward the triumphant ending in the third, to soar and be filled with emotion, to listen with the large organ of the whole body. I learned that the concerto was the conversation between the solitary voice of the instrument and the orchestra, metaphor of the Great Conversation of life. It was all innocent, the beauty pouring into my wide eyes and my bone-knowing. And the hungry turning of the glossy pages of the orange book. We hear these pieces, these old friends, again and again, recited to us by interpreters who bring us back to indivisible essentials captured in those capsules of perfection.

If there were ever to be a soundtrack of those four years in Iran, it would be Rachmaninov's second piano concerto. I listened to the recording we owned—another one now lost to me—so many times that it has been difficult to listen to any other version whose even slightly differing tempi are jarring to my ears, skewing the weight of those sweeping emotions, chords of catastrophic gloom. But it has been difficult to listen to any version at all. Even past my immediate rejection of tempi, the music transports me straight back to a world crumbling before my eyes, the weight of my adolescence without guidance in matters of puberty and boys, a home undergoing seismic shifts, a people on alert, murdered, humiliated in coerced public confessions, women disfigured by acid thrown in their faces for reasons ranging from improper *hejab* to the audacity of visibility in society.

Rachmaninov's second piano concerto is for me all these emotions pent-up, of my being rewarded for being a *Good Girl* and doing housework when my mother was on periods of bed rest in her turmoil for having been born in the wrong time and place without a channel for the expression of these truths. Rachmaninov's second piano concerto is my people's anguish passed on to me. But mostly, it is my own loss of innocence. My own transformation from child to having-seen.

There was in my father's demeanor, behind the silences, an unspoken kind of demand, an invisible pressure cooker of expectation of something undefinable, a fulfillment of some moral obligation I owed to the universe.

On October 6, 1983, Shamlou's candidacy for the Nobel Prize in Literature was announced.

My family left Iran in March 1984, spent six months in France, and eventually settled in the United States.

7. THE NEW WORLD

GROCERY SUPERSTORES WERE ONE OF THE SEVEN WONDERS of the World. I had never seen *any* store, *anywhere* with these proportions. Vons, Albertsons, Alpha Beta, I marveled at them all: rows and rows of products, brand name after brand name. So many different tubes of toothpaste to choose from.

I developed an obsession with Kraft cream cheese, instant cheesecake in graham-cracker crust with canned cherry topping, and Minute Made orange juice. All-American foods, nothing like the homemade, wholesome foods I came from. None of these American foods were safe in the refrigerator in my aunt's house—where we lived for the first year—and for some time both families were gripped with a mystery juice-drinker who would empty within a matter of hours a carton of juice meant for two families of four, drinking from the carton with the fridge door open, hand on the handle. I was soon discovered and given a talking-to about being measured and frugal.

The radio alarm clock blared Eurythmics and George Michael with WHAM! at 7 a.m. *Wake me up, before you go go! 'Cause I'm not planning on going solo.* My cousin, in whose bedroom I slept, and who was halfway ready by 7:15 while I was still fast asleep, would shout, irritated:

GET UP! NILOU! GET UP!

I was on the floor, wrapped in a sleeping bag, the zipper indenting my cheek.

So this was America. I had seen it five years earlier, but I was so young then and happy to watch TV lying on my stomach on the thick beige carpet of the empty wooden house, and sit awkwardly in the sixth grade class where I didn't understand why the students were sitting around tables of four like in a restaurant. This time, I looked outside the windows at the foggy mornings before being driven to high school in the rolling suburban maze. I had no sense of the nearby Pacific Ocean yet. No sense of the outlet.

In Europe, it was even harder to be comfortable. You always had to be so sophisticated and polished to fit in. They were not kidding about old-world Europe.

We learned our lesson: We strolled in the streets all day and thought we could shop for food after 5 p.m. on a Saturday (forget Sundays). But the doors wouldn't open, reflecting instead our bewildered squinting faces stuck to the glass. Doors shut to us as if to say, *You don't know our ways, you are not welcome.*

Oh, God, why did we have to try to push the door open?! Now everyone knows we didn't know!

In Europe, you had to tap into your most bourgeois and then some. In America, those bourgeois ways just made you look even more foreign.

So this was America:

Coral-colored tiled roofs — *So European.*

New, man-made lake — *I don't understand.*

The smell of Dep on eighties hairdos — *Everyone is so morning-fresh here.*

Lockers in hallways! — *Steno and Mead notebooks.*

Cheerleaders — *Oh, my god, their koochies are exposed!*

Pep rallies for home games — *What?*

Baskin-Robbins and 31 Flavors — *So many flavors, but so artificial tasting.*

I stand up at attention when teacher walks in, others put their flip-flopped feet up and chew gum — *Americans have no manners?*

They know nothing about geography — *BOOOO, I RAN DOWN THE STREET, AYATOLLAH!*

No one talks to me but immigrants, exchange students, and my cousin — *I am not a popular girl back in Tehran anymore.*

Spanish street names — *What are these words?*

Thankfully, I had speed-learned some Spanish with a tutor, the language I had elected as my third language in my partial sophomore year in France, just as I had learned French with a tutor in Iran. I had asked my parents to be taught Azeri Turkish, the native language of my grandparents on both sides who came from the Iranian state of Azerbaijan. *Yes, sure,* but my parents took me to a French tutor instead. We knocked on a door and an overly made-up bottle-blonde with very wide hips opened. *Bonjour! I am your French teacher!* We already owned my textbook, *Cours de Langue et Civilisation Française* by C. Mauger, my mother's old and frayed copy. The tutor had married an Iranian man and made the move to live a nice life in the East. Was she an expatriate or immigrant or refugee? She was a former equestrian—still dressed as one—who attributed her very wide hips to having stopped being one.

It would be years before I would understand the history of the genocide that is California, the United States, the erasure behind the sleepy rolling hills and pleasant-sounding names of Mission Viejo, Vista del Lago, Capistrano, Costa Mesa, Corona del Mar, Los Angeles, Las Palmas, Malibu, Santa Barbara, San Luis Obispo, Los Gatos, San Francisco, Sacramento, Lake Tahoe, Mount Tamalpais, Tucson, Tacoma, Seattle, Potomac, Denali, Utah, Alaska, Iowa, Idaho, Sandusky, Waco, Wichita, Chattanooga, Tennessee, Kentucky, Winona, Winnipesaukee, Pough-keepsie, Poconos, Mojave, Miami, Michigan, Chicago, Cheyenne, Shenandoah, Algonquin, Manhattan. America.

In college, our willingness toward madness, to experience it all, was the link of camaraderie between us few misfits who clung together, making declarations, expressing outrage, professing blood-bonds. We stepped easily over the line of boundaries we did not have at the drop of a hat. While the rest of our generation was dutifully following safe paths, even against their natures, we were on the fringes experiencing the unnamed things we knew existed below the surface of things, unconcerned about our futures, deferring them by virtue of an unspoken faith we had in life somehow working out in what seemed eons away.

Now, thirty years later, after having done what I've wanted, carved the path that has led me here, where I sit and write you at this very moment, I realize that it is no wonder why so many people my age are restless, searching for something that they must feel they've lost, or never found, or never touched. I think it's the freedom and abandon they did not grant themselves in those formative years, while they were busy being industrious, finishing degrees and starting career paths, pleasing parents, checking off accomplishments on that imaginary list of life's milestones. They missed out on the wandering years, those early adulthood years.

My solace in this sober adulthood, in this tedium of deadlines and tasks and obligations and masks and pretenses of authority, is that I was once wholly wild, heedless, unrestrained, moneyless, unbothered to *secure* a future. As I struggle with emotional blocks and malaise, the difficulty of living with the erasures that others have tried their best to perpetrate upon me, and the weight of rapidly disappearing time, I find solace in knowing that I made deposits of experience in the bank account of my life. No one can artificially manufacture that currency after the fact, nor strip me from mine. I feel that and only that affords me the ability to carry on in the face of life's difficulties. Had I not availed myself of the luxury of recklessness, of experiences, had I tamed myself in favor of mores, conventions, and manners, had I bent to the official script, I, too, would feel unfathomable emptiness inside me now, a void much worse than a self-conscious state of hollowness, but rather a numbness that does not know it is emptiness eating away at the core, an odorless gas that unsuspectedly seizes and kills before you know it. I see this numbness around me everywhere, humans living like automata, the walking dead. When the end arrives, there would be no time to replenish the life force, to rectify the unlived life.

My journal entries for a decade and a half would mainly center on my yearning to know the Truth, the stripped-down Truth of everything.

I dropped out of college during my sophomore year, no longer on the medical school track, and waitressing, to my mother's horror, living aimlessly. My father self-banished to freezing, lonesome apartments wherever there was opportunity to fulfill requirements of foreign-educated physicians toward a medical license in the U.S. It was the equivalent of enduring medical school, residency, and a fellowship all over again in his forties and fifties, after having already practiced for two decades as a sought-after surgeon in Iran. He frequently laments those lost years when he did not see his children. I was ousted from our home, living on empty near the beach. My mother worked in the same neighborhood, and I saw her on the streets. Sometimes we passed each other like acquaintances. I do not remember where my brother pursued his education, plotting to leave the trenches of loss. I re-enrolled as a Comparative Literature major in 1989. When immigrant parents say they sacrificed it all for their children, they truly did.

It seemed uncanny that as I journey back to the inceptions of me, I should see the 2017 film, *Poesía Sin Fin,* or *Endless Poetry* in English, Alejandro Jodorowsky's autobiographical film about growing up to become an artist. This still is from a scene where a young poet-artist bursts into a café, her entrance arresting the film's protagonist sitting at the bar on the right, on the brink of releasing himself from the bonds of a suppressive upbringing and discovering his own art. He is bedazzled by the rare and ferocious creature, and embarks on a tumultuous adventure with her, his every horizon extending in her company.

I immediately felt her untamed spirit on a visceral level, but it wasn't until afterward, when my friend Roy named her *Niloufar Talebi,* that it instantly gelled, and I recognized myself in her and her in myself, that unbridled girl I remember being in my early twenties. The character in the film instantly entered my DNA, her abandon to her promptings, the declamation of ideals, the extremes of opinion, the ferocity, and under the stormy armor, a vulnerable person looking to be understood, loved. And from that moment on, this very image became, retroactively, the embodiment of how I had lived, who I had been.

And just like that, the future illuminated the past. An image recovered, awakened a past that had burrowed in a remote part of my body. Or rather, a long-buried layer was invoked, reimagined, seen from the vantage of now, of art. I had burst into my life declaring, protesting, searching, screaming.

This is more or less who I was when Shamlou visited me in 1990.

During his 1990–1991 tour of the United States, Shamlou held several talks and readings, including at UCLA and UC Berkeley. One of the talks at Berkeley was titled, "My Worries," in which he pointed to the role that keeping the masses ignorant plays in the enabling of tyrants, his chief concern throughout his life.

But he seems to have gone a bit too far for what the Iranian public could handle. He eventually arrived at the tenth century tome, the *Shahnameh,* or *The Epic of Persian Kings*, composed by the Persian poet Ferdowsi and widely revered by Iranians as their national epic. The *Shahnameh* was composed three hundred years after the seventh century invasion of Arabs who brought Islam to the Persian empire and "diluted" the Persian language and culture with theirs. Ferdowsi, who was from the landed gentry class, dedicated thirty years of his life to composing the *Shahnameh*. Shamlou focused on the story of Zahhak, a foreign king— an Arab perhaps?—who is portrayed as a despotic serpent king, against whom the working classes eventually revolt. In his talk, Shamlou cautioned against a nationalist reading of the stories and mythologies versified in the tome, characterizing it as a tool for nationalist agendas and the perpetual empowering of tyrants.

This did not go well with the Iranian immigrant community, who desperately need to root their identity in something grand, nothing short of a very big book about Persian heroes and victorious battles against Arabs. *Rah, Rah, Persian Pride* is what they want, not a prodding of their inferiority complex. Of all the controversial statements Shamlou made—and there were many, including the article he wrote about traditional Persian music being a dead and non-innovative art form he wanted nothing to do with—this one seemed to have alienated his own people for many years to come.

In 2013, after I presented my translations of Shamlou's work at a program at the Hammer Museum in Los Angeles, while receiving compliments in the lobby from an elated audience, a group of Iranian men approached me. After a quick congratulations, the tallest one's eyes suddenly became possessed, he foamed at the mouth, cheek muscles twitching as he wagged his index finger in my face and shrieked, *But Shamlou was a traitor to Iran and should never be mentioned!* I'm glad I had the presence of mind to *woman up* and shake an index finger back up at him, saying in a more possessed voice, *This is neither the time nor the place to have this conversation*, and walked away. They stood there dazed and confused. *Yes, that's right, I, a petite woman, just told you off.* Later I discovered videos of grown men, breathless, speechless on their self-produced, DIY, satellite cable "shows" fiercely waving the Shah's royalist flag and crying, *Iran, Iran, our Iran*, and, *What has Shamlou done to our* Shahnameh, *that traitor!*

This photo of a man pointing his finger in my face and reprimanding me was taken years earlier, around 2006, just after I had performed my translations of contemporary Iranian poets from my anthology, *Belonging: New Poetry by Iranians Around the World*, at a festival, coincidentally called "Poetry That is Life," after Shamlou's poem. The man, who seemed to have psychological problems, came up afterwards and yelled nonsensical things at me. I don't know who snapped this shot and why. I just stood there, letting him blow off steam, because we women learn early on to protect our bodies, to let the man calm himself down while we take the abuse. But I did not take it in 2013. I growled back at the tall men besieging me. In 2018, I am finishing this book to exorcise even greater brutalities. The future is only looking up for me.

Poetry That is Life

Los Angeles — April 25, 1990

Backstage at UCLA's Royce Hall, I watch Shamlou being wheeled onto the large stage. Later, I slip him a note as he is helped into the Mercedes-Benz driving him away.

Is this why he later came to visit me, so out of his way? Or was it because his entourage, who had read my long automatic writing piece, had reported to Shamlou that I was a young writer on the rise. I had sat for hours at gatherings in Shamlou's honor all over California, sitting at his feet, inhaling it all, taking notes, this time as an artist, my stakes so different, even more venerating of the God of Literature.

I have since stepped onto that same UCLA stage myself to present Shamlou's poetry in my translation. The backstage area still seemed as expansive as it did in 1990 when I was in Shamlou's party.

The folded note said, *I love you very much!*

This must have been a summoning of sorts to him.

Laguna Beach, CA — November 1990

I receive the poet in the afternoon
in my dusty rose crepe and satin sleeveless
tank flowing over matching long skirt
reserved and dignified
on the sofa with floral upholstery in other people's living
room where I was living.

So proper sit pupil and mentor at forty-five-degree angle toward each other.
He's here because mutual friends have read my
writing influenced by the surrealists
and told him, *Niloufar is at a critical juncture in her life becoming a writer*,
or some such thing,
and she needs you.

Semi-jokingly he asks, *What is wrong*,
seeing what artist-in-the-becoming pain he can fix
having had people drive him for two hours to stay for one.

When I call him *Amoo* Shamlou—Uncle Shamlou
—he insists I not call him that, says it makes him feel five million years old
smiling with his aquatic mammal mouth
(he was 65)
and he reaches out
I wanted to smoke, but he took my cigarette away.

I CANNOT REMEMBER WHAT HE SAID (something In Praise of
Beauty, about a fire that ignites the wet logs of the heart when others
douse it, about love that is not out of need being pure).

I CANNOT REMEMBER WHAT I SAID.

I CANNOT REMEMBER his phone calls afterward.

Fail, memory.

I do remember walking on the beach with my best friend soon afterward, waves crashing over our words.

I have read of other people's fateful meetings with Shamlou, eloquent weaver of endless anecdotes, bewitcher of captive audiences. I have listened as Mrs. Shamlou told me about Shamlou talking about everything and anything on their park bench. But I do not need these anecdotes. I know this firsthand.

My "Shamlou" has been a feeling, a phantom, a mystery. A genius of discipline, a committed warrior. He is my parents' guest of honor, the poet-jester who drank and howled and held court. He is the disc jockey of the music of my life. He is the stories he told, the books he gave me. He is the old man we helped float in our home swimming pool. He is the stories his widow told me about their lives. He is the cultural giant whose work I toil to read, the subject of my research, the author of words I translate and the worlds I discover. He is the fearless dissident, the speaker being wheeled onto a grand stage. He is the chain smoker with a voice like none other. He is the voice of recitations in my earbuds. He is the unguarded poet who came to see how he could help me that afternoon, an old man who wanted to feel young again, he is a symbol of freedom, breaker of boundaries, the pushing past of expectations, he is grit in the face of suffering for the vision one invents. He is the feeling of all possibilities, of flight. The champion of inventing language for one's relationship to the world. Of living this brief life to its core. All of these exist as the composite Shamlou of my life.

My Shamlou is mine, no one else's. He cracked open the universe to me. I came away from examining him closely awed by the capacity of the human form when it takes on mythic proportions, and enlightened to giants in their human form. There were gifts in looking up to him as a God of Literature, and there were epiphanies in breaking him down to his mortal components.

I had erased myself almost entirely from this book. Drop by drop, I had to insinuate myself in. To be the *me* in a m…me…memoir. Mirror.

I drifted for a few years after graduating from college, a less than stellar feat that took no less than seven years, two major changes, at least two long breaks in the middle, and many moves, subsisting on not much more than my convictions and ideals. Toward the end, I began working at Rizzoli Bookstore, where I ordered the international magazines and newspapers, took advantage of a steady supply of books and an eclectic selection of CDs from their music department, crossed paths with interesting and multilingual people, and kept myself alive. It was a stimulating and easy job, but not a future.

In my time off, I made the rounds to my old jaunts, the college library, the campus cafés, loitering around the humanities building where I had taken class, the art department where I had painted, done performance art, fallen in love, and attended student shows and gallery openings, all of us students donning airs of insecurities, to eat and drink from the measly opening night spreads and sit around and chain smoke, theorizing about this and that. Driving around from place to place, aimless, plan-less, I almost never ran into anyone I knew, or experienced a substantial conversation. I recognized fewer and fewer faces over time as they graduated and went on to their next steps, graduate school, medical school, careers, fellowships, travel.

Alone, I was hungry for a union that would spark something, be the key piece in the puzzle of my directionless life, whose only thing going for it was a structureless but creative set of projects I had fallen into after a chance meeting at the bookstore with a biochemist who turned out to be a world-renowned scientist and ethnobotanist. At the bookstore, he asked for a book on medicinal herbs, and when I reacted with interest in the occult and the healing power of plants, he flipped his card onto the counter and told me to visit him at his office on campus in one month, after he returned from Borneo. I later learned that he had co-developed the discipline of and coined the term *zoopharmacognosy*, the study of how non-human animals self-medicate by selecting and using plants to treat and prevent disease. Dr. Rodriguez studied primates all over the world.

When I followed up and visited him in his office, I was met with a professor in a white lab coat in a long trailer of a lab bustling with a throng of revering graduate students, at once responding to overseas phone calls and faxes, doling out instructions, and conducting an interrupted yet laser-sharp interrogation of me. During that first visit, he showed me his butterfly room, a cool and silent sanctuary where fluttered hundreds of rare butterflies. He asked me what I wanted to do with my life, because working in a bookstore was not it. I said I wanted to write. He rhapsodized about books and films and art, and I realized I was in the presence of a visionary. He detected my similar affinities for art, said writing I should do, and then arranged to put me on his payroll. For two years I was a commissioned creative.

This meant that I had a university car, which came with state tags and parking privileges, when I needed to drive to Los Angeles or anywhere farther than the vicinity of campus to gather information. It meant I met him for extended lunches during which he spun stories from his adventures. I traveled to Mexico, New Mexico, New York, and other places where he thought I might find the conferences in which he was taking part informative. So much hunger for life radiated out of him.

I joined him at *mercados* in Mexico as he probed and smelled and tasted plants. We attended native healing ceremonies, watched shamans and *curanderas* making ritual. There was no expectation of me, just that my own cultural observations and research into medicinal plants would lead to writing a series of children's stories for his summer science camp for underprivileged Latino kids, what he himself had been in south Texas before pulling himself up by the bootstraps. But he never forced a deadline or output onto me otherwise.

It was a creative person's dream. To be paid to expand in one's own direction. His administrative staff treated me with suspicion. They thought I must be having some kind of affair with their boss to be given these unusual and undefined privileges, something they could not understand, not in the hard and measured world of academia and scientific research. Eventually, everything coalesced, and on the weekend before the science camp, two stories came out of me I do not know where from because I just wrote them down. And I joined the camp classrooms to offer a bookmaking arts and crafts workshop based on the stories. The kids' projects were displayed during a Hispanic Heritage event on campus. I taped and displayed them on the walls of the nearest building. I had also enlisted someone to edit the video footage I took of the process, the professor's vision, interviews with the kids' parents, showing the impact of arts education in young people's lives.

This was the documentary whose master copy I was turning in on the day of my car accident in August 1994 on the 405 freeway during which I knew I was moving to San Francisco, which I did in December 1994.

8. TEHRAN

"The past changes as one advances."

— Italo Calvino, *Invisible Cities*

I READ SOMEWHERE THAT TO LOVE SOMEONE is to put yourself in their place, their story, and figure out how to tell yourself in their story. I tried to locate Shamlou's story. Two opposites came to the fore: the beloved's spirit changes one's DNA, but also, the beloved is a projection of one's self already formed at birth.

In search of Shamlou and myself in the streets of Tehran, I open a new browser window with trepidation, knowing that to Google Map Tehran was the opening of a Pandora's box of suppressed emotions, hazy memories that would not be reassembled, endless questions that would never be answered, and finally, of helplessness, and the festering of subdued fury at the inability to return to the city of my Creation Story, my Dublin of Leopold Bloom, my Paris of Hemingway, my London of Oliver Twist, my city that faded to me long ago, now invisible to me, or rather, I invisible to it. I turn the invisibility into a center of infinite potential, what Marco Polo did to the cities in Kublai Khan's vast empire.

The land of Iran is in the shape of a sitting cat, bearing the Caspian Sea on its back, and perching in the south on the Persian Gulf. The Alborz mountain range would line up as the cat's spinal cord, spanning west to east from the border of Azerbaijan in the west along the southern coast of the Caspian Sea south of the Russian border to the eastern borders of Iran. I lived in the capital city of Tehran, on the southern slopes of the mountain range, which divides two climates—subtropical states to the north, and cold, semi-arid Tehran to the south. The Alborz mountains, ridged with snow, loom large in the distance of Tehran.

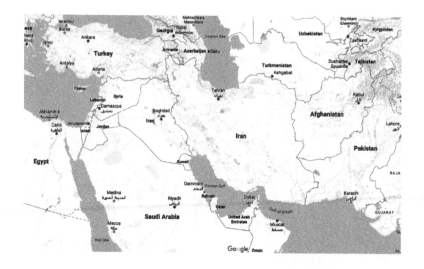

I never saw anything south of Tehran, not the two deserts, not the Zoroastrian Towers of Silence for the excoriation of the dead in the central province of Yazd, not Shiraz, the ancient capital city of Persia near the ruins of Persepolis, not the Hellenistic ruins of structures built after the invasion of Alexander the Great. I never reached the Persian Gulf to hear African-inspired folk music, a legacy of slavery, the continent of Africa just southwest of the Persian Gulf, beyond Saudi Arabia and the Red Sea, which Moses crossed in the Biblical account of the Exodus while escaping the Egyptians. My family hails from the state of Azerbaijan in the northwest, the head of the cat. I did see Tabriz, capital of Eastern Azerbaijan, but I was only a toddler then. I never saw Urmia, capital of Western Azerbaijan, nor Lake Urmia nestled between the two provinces, the salty lake where my arthritic grandmother, a child-bride, is said to have found relief floating.

I look up Shamlou's addresses, the streets of his funeral procession. In a flood of curiosity, I look up my own addresses. Street and neighborhood names changed after the revolution, so progress was slow. Suddenly, I am possessed with place. Having been away from Iran for more than three decades, I spent weeks on Google Maps, but in the end, how impossible it was to grasp the proportions of one's childhood. Even searching for walking and driving directions and noting distances between our places, startlingly shorter than expected, I could not capture the exact dimensions of my childhood in our city, Tehran. Shamlou had said that things cannot be captured, for in the seeking, there is only more seeking stretching into the vast horizon of the future.

I searched in books, in dusty, musty, old papers,
in my remembrances
I searched for myself and tomorrow in a memory that
no longer serves
Astonishing! I am an explorer
not the explored
I am here, and the future is in my fists.[6]

I do know, however, that my blue bedroom in Tehran, where I was nightly the solitary mariner of a little boat-bed in the great stormy ocean of its beyond, which faced the tall and narrow wooden closet that receded into hyperspace where bogeymen lurked awaiting like a genie in Aladdin's lamp the slightest crack in its door to pounce at me, where I kept girlish trinkets at my DIY dressing table and bench made of the sturdy foam packing of my father's medical instruments that arrived at our home address and that my mother beautified with a ruffled blue cover she sewed, next to the mighty grown-up desk, behind which I sat diligently night after night on a chair with high armrests to pursue scholarship with my back to the window portal through which the wonder of the city sky and silent snowfall entered my pen, was a small room. I can see it now, skewed in perspective the way Van Gogh's blue bedroom is depicted in his 1889 painting, *Bedroom in Arles*, and in scale the way objects and furniture enlarge and shrink in illogical proportions in *Personal Values,* Magritte's 1952 painting of a bedroom with its interior walls painted in his signature blue sky and fluffy white clouds. My blue bedroom is my palace of memories.

To build a map of Shamlou's Tehran, I searched for his birth home, the home where he and Aida met as neighbors, the cafés and restaurants he visited, various addresses of his temporary lodgings, his last home numbered 555 in Karaj where he died, the route of his funeral procession, his resting place. He was human after all, he hauled belongings and moved, he walked to meetings books in hand, married three times and fathered four children, maybe fled from back doors of domiciles in night-raids, went to bed in despair, in hunger, spent years imprisoned. He was said to smell of ink from toiling for bread at various printing presses. He walked to cafés to meet other writers, retreated for lunch and conversation to friends' homes, found peace in homes Aida set up to keep him grounded, protected, worry-free, to hunch over papers and books night and day toward building a monumental legacy, producing works that are still being edited for future publication.

Poring over the map of Tehran, I saw district names, street names, landmarks, park names, many of which were familiar. The names are spelled out on Google Maps in both Persian and English transliteration. In which language was I to relate to these names? The spelling out of these places in these two languages seemed disconnected from my relationship to the actual places, which are yet more disconnected in space.

I have spoken English my entire life, having been born in London, but my surrender to English as an expatriate overrides the English that one speaks as a second language. English seems native to me now as much as my native tongue feels foreign to me. The languages are liquid now like ocean meeting ocean.

Going between Google Maps and Google Images, I proceeded to reconstruct my own youth, the route to my father's clinic and hospital, the streets I used to walk with my mother, hand in hand, to visit him at work. Streets that led to pastry shops, my mother's museums of earthly delights, to my piano lessons when I was so young and my mother would hail taxis with me in her arms, to my mother's tailors' ateliers where I sat in those shaded private homes in unfamiliar quarters watching the catwalk as a—I now realize—gay man called Essi, a feminine diminutive for the male name, Esmail, the equivalent of Ishmael of *Moby Dick* fame, fitted my mother in an endless parade of dresses, obsessed alongside my mother with the lace color, the fabric, the buttons, the zippers, the patterns taken from *Burda,* the holy bible of style magazines that contained patterns for the designs in its issues, which we used to receive from overseas.

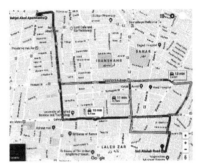 

I zoomed in and out infinite times, toggled between satellite and street views. I searched for my own markers, Ettefagh school, the Armenian cathedral, Saint Sarkis, close to the Behjat Abad apartment complex where we lived both before and after the revolution from the late 1970s to the early 1980s, where Shamlou had first visited us. In the 1940s, Behjat Abad was at the northern edge of the Armenian district of Tehran around *Bahar* street, which explains the presence of Saint Sarkis cathedral, and possibly why Aida's family lived nearby, next to Shamlou's mother's house. In my time, the Behjat Abad complex was one of the first high-rise apartments built in the center of the city. Now the neighborhood offers Asian products, the closest thing to a Chinatown Tehran has. Our apartment was a three-bedroom, two-bathroom, first-floor unit divided into a family living room where the television was across from sofas covered in rough and itchy brown fabric where the Shamlou literary crowd was generally entertained, which bled into the guest living room with a sofa in light green upholstery, and a dining room between the guest living room and the kitchen. We had a trash chute inside the bathroom near the entrance doorway, the corner of the apartment where it seemed to be forever an arctic winter.

I discovered that our apartment was shockingly close, a fifteen-minute walk to south *Kheradmand* street where Shamlou and Aida had been neighbors when Shamlou was living at his mother's house for a time when they met in the spring of 1962. Their official meeting date, the 14th of *Farvardin*, April 4, is the day after the festivities of *Nowruz*, the Persian New Year on the vernal equinox. Shamlou's birthplace at 134 Safi Alishah road was only a little farther away southeast of Kheradmand street. Some of Shamlou's other locations, homes where he had stayed after returning from abroad and before settling back in Tehran, were also not too far off.

I was astonished to find these proximities, connections made on a static map so many years later. Does this kind of geography carry as much meaning to a dweller of Tehran as it does to me now so far away in time and space?

These virtual voyages through sepia, black and white, and new, color images of Tehran suddenly make me *feel* something bone-deep. Perhaps as a reaction against otherness and the burden and confusion of claiming and defending an IDENTITY, the affliction of the exiled, allegiances of such nature previously eluded me. Maybe I intentionally avoided a garden-variety nostalgia for my homeland in order to survive the grips of chronic sickness if I allowed it to penetrate my body and deposit itself in the history of my non-belonging. I have had to shed much, left with no choice but to fling myself into an orbit of strength, that moat we dig between us and the world to buffer us against our deepest hurt, those red wounds.

But in what feels like peeping on my own Iran, in the fondness for those semi-familiar names as I try to associate an image, even a blurry snapshot, to them, or determine whether I had frequented those places, and if so, what could have brought me to those streets, that I *feel* my ancestry, blood, tribe. I discover that I am, or was, but am Iranian.

Even more. Tehranian.

Tehran, capital city of nearly nine million. Tehran, city that did not exist when Alexander the Great conquered the Persian Empire in 332 BC, Tehran, city that did not exist when Islam traveled east from its birthplace of Saudi Arabia to Persia in the seventh century, Tehran, city that did not exist when Genghis Khan pillaged Asia in his Mongol invasion. Tehran, city first chosen as the capital of Persia in 1796 during the Qajar reign.

Tehran, lit city, city of four seasons, hilly city sloping down the foothills of the great Alborz mountain range with rivers and mineral hot springs, crowned by the snow-capped peak of Mount Damavand, a potentially active volcano at 18,406 feet, the highest peak in Iran, the highest volcano in Asia, the second most prominent in Asia after Mount Everest, and the twelfth most prominent peak in the world. Tehran, city of steep northern streets at the foothills, flood-prone metropolis over a bed of active fault lines.

Mount Damavand occupies a special place in the Iranian literary and mythical imagination, the site of many battles, retreats, and imprisonments. The mountain is said to hold magical powers in Ferdowsi's *Shahnameh*, the verse collection of creation stories of early humans, the Persian people, and the heroes who protect the empire on through the conquest of Alexander the Great in 332 BC, and a quasi-historical account of the empire up to the Islamic conquest of Persia in the seventh century.

The *Shahnameh* is a tome of fathers betraying sons, kingdoms their heroes. Damavand is home to the mighty mythical bird, Simorgh, its guardian who mothered the albino infant Prince Zal after he is abandoned in the mountains. Zal grows into a noble man, is returned to humanity, and becomes the father of Iran's legendary hero, Rostam. Simorgh's golden feather saved Rostam in his trial against another epic hero, Esfandiar, who was made invincible by the prophet Zoroaster with magical armor and chain. In the battle, Rostam is wounded and retreats to dress his wounds. He summons Simorgh by burning one of her golden feathers given to him. Simorgh heals Rostam and his horse, and informs Rostam of the secret to killing Esfandiar—his Achilles' heel is his eyes—with a double-headed arrow, which Rostam does. While dying, Esfandiar asks Rostam not to blame himself, the blame being with his own father for forcing him to fight Rostam, a doomed situation according to the oracle. Shamlou ties in this reference with Abraham's trial by fire in his poem, *"Abraham in Flames."*

Damavand is also a symbol of Iranian resistance against tyranny and colonialism. The three-headed dragon, Azi Dahaka, was chained at Damavand to remain there until the end of time. In other versions of the legend, the foreign tyrant Zahhak, the serpent king, was chained in a cave in the mountain after being defeated by the rebels, Kaveh and Fereydoun. It is also the place Fereydoun took refuge when he was chased by Zahhak's spies. The Alborz mountains are the dwelling of Kai Kobad before being summoned to the throne of Iran by Rostam, as well as the homeland of Keyumars, the first human according to the creation myth. Finally, Mount Damavand is the location from which the legendary hero archer, Arash, shot his magical arrow to mark the border of Iran.

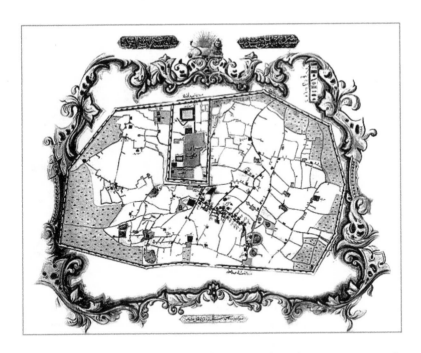

Tehran had a twelve-mile circumference and twelve gates in 1926, around the time of the coronation of Reza Khan, whom Vita Sackville-West called in her travelogue-memoir, a glimpse into Orientalized Iran, *Passenger to Teheran*, "the Cossack trooper with a brutal jaw," much to the dismay of her husband, Harold Nicolson, a British diplomat to Iran who served Reza Khan.

Tehran, spelled over the centuries with the two different Ts in the Persian alphabet, تهران and طهران. Tehran, city of crown jewels and royal complexes with lush gardens, city of old horse- and donkey-drawn trolleys, of crumbling façades and ruins, relics from the devastating eight-year Iran-Iraq war. Tehran, crossroad city of many tongues and faces left over from Silk Road caravans, Tehran, city of historic gates, *darvazeh*, ancient edifices, Shah Abdol-Azim to the south, Ghazvin or Ghadimi to the west, through which peasants on foot searched for a better life, arcs under which my own ancestors entered, gateways into new worlds. Perhaps the poet who lifted himself out of the bleak circumstances of his life and disrupted the status quo also graced these gates.

Tehran, city of soot landing silently like snow on the shoulder of my mother's sleeve as she is gingerly exiting the passenger side of our car impeccably dressed and with hands held at attention, fingertips glistening with fresh red polish, soot which she delicately blows off the cream-colored silk and then boasts to my father of her ingenious calculation against the error of a rub-off that would have ruined the pristine surface with a black and red streak.

Tehran, city of slogans, of festivals and cinemas, city of grand, tree-lined boulevards, city of sycamores and elms, of shaded alleys of no significance, city of storytellers in tea houses of working-class districts and wandering showmen of olden days with their "European City" peep boxes, *shahre-farang*, made of metal in the shape of an oriental castle with several holes through which images transported crouching viewers to exotic lands they could never visit, Tehran, city of summer siestas, my head on the bare, clammy torso of my father home for lunch from the clinic, city of uniformed schoolchildren running to buses or cars, Tehran, city of child laborers and child beggars and street vendors squatting in cardboard boxes, sleeping alone on sidewalks, not immune to extortion by officials to allow them, city of bewildered peasants hanging themselves under bridges, impoverished from the confiscation of their livelihoods by the authorities who rob their provincial dreams, Tehran, city of the sick and addicted cowering behind burning trash bins, splayed in toxic alleys, Tehran, city of southern slums and shanty towns with bitter graffiti that reads, "Don't look, it will cost you too much," Tehran, city of hungry grave-dwellers, of sewer-pipe-undesirables with gangrened or frostbitten feet, outcasts of tin-town settlements I beheld in horror from the car on the way to the great cemetery of the south, *Zahra's Paradise*, to watch my mother weep at my grandmother Zahra's grave.

Tehran, city of the discarded and forgotten, city of gutters, cruel city into whose eyes I cannot look.

Tehran, tinsel city of mullah money, oil money, city of Instagrammed nose jobs, flaunted Fendi bags, gangster hip-hop poses and underground jam sessions, secret city of pool parties and catwalks, city of ski trips and chalets, designer vodkas and supercars, depravity and decadence, no different than Bel Air.

Tehran, city of educated women, vanguard warriors of the streets, war paint on the canvas of their faces—the legally visible body part—city of uprisings, city of the endless gaze of the Green Movement's fallen Neda, city in which I was apprehended, Tehran, city of unveiled lionesses waving their peace flags of a veil on a stick standing silently on utility platforms on busy streets to protest compulsory *hejab,* lionesses whose legs break when pushed off by angry men, Tehran, city of big brother and sister morality police, of detention centers and torture chambers, city of the disappeared, of discarded corpses, city of forced confessions and prison suicides.

Tehran, city of universities and publishing houses and taxis and traffic, city of convertible drives to the Caspian Sea with screaming cousins, city of bazaars and malls and markets, of museums and bridges, city of citizens in amusement parks hollering on harrowing joy rides, Tehran, city of twenty-one hundred parks and family outings, city of a New York High Line–style *Nature Bridge* designed by a twenty-six-year-old Iranian woman, city of selfies with friends, city of stylish restaurants with international foods, chic coffee shops with hookahs, quaint restaurants with light blue windows, city of fortune-tellers, city of superhighways and rivers and boardwalks, of mosques and temples and churches, of airports and modern towers.

Tehran, city of unmet desires, of park benches where Shamlou spoke for hours to the mesmerized young Aida, city of inner courtyards, city of Nima and his door, city in whose bustling streets I held my mother's hand and collided with workers and their gamey scent of cigarette breath, Ramadan fasting breath, alcohol hangovers, infrequent showers, smells whose potency escalated in the summer months.

Tehran, city of Café Naderi, the legendary intellectual's cafe of the Modernist era, and the only coffee shop to be registered as a site of national heritage, where poets and literati, including a young Shamlou, were spotted reading, discussing, and plotting the literary future of Iran. Café Naderi, the Café Sperl of Vienna, the Les Deux Magots of Paris.

Café Naderi, established in 1927 by an Armenian immigrant, its adjacent Naderi Hotel, and its owner in dispute with city officials for intending to separate the café and hotel rather than restore the buildings.

Tehran, city in which the house at 134 Safi Alishah road is no longer. Or perhaps an abandoned building spotted nearby is Shamlou's birthplace. A nation does not know. The offices of the famous *Khoosheh* magazine, where Shamlou was editor-in-chief, his office housing a long table at which editorial meetings were held across from the managing editor's office, and where he returned twelve years later to save the publication, is no longer. Neither is the Safi Alishah bookstore. The two adjacent buildings just off south Kheradmand street where Shamlou and Aida were neighbors in 1962, one a two-story brick building and the other a four-story apartment building with a white stone façade, could be cultural sites, but are not accessible to the public. A house at the corner of *Villa* and *Khosrow* streets, where Shamlou lived for some time in the 1960s and where the poem *"Aida in the Mirror"* came to him in the middle of the night after a rainstorm, which he transcribed on the wall because he could not find paper, is abandoned.

Tehran, city of erasures, neglected cultural history. What replaces is amnesia. One day, there will be no sign or memory of the pre-1979 Iran that I knew, the city of a golden youth spent in three neighborhoods that demarcated three phases of my life before the age of fifteen when I left Iran for the last time.

There is a Tehran in my mind. I do not know if it bears any resemblance to the Tehran that exists. It is the composite city of the remote past, my own past when it was my present, and the city of now I only know from afar, in fragments, virtually. It is cities erased and cities erected to make the city of my imagination. It is the Orientalist city captured, romanticized, minimized, and gazed upon by the Western eye, the city I saw with my own eyes both before and after the revolution, the city captured in dazzling photographs of the Anglo-Russian Invasion of Iran, the city of the 1953 coup d'état against Prime Minister Mossadegh for nationalizing Iran's own oil, the city of black-and-white images by Antoin Sevruguin capturing the turn from the Victorian to the Modern era, the city in which I kissed a boy in the basement wearing a floral green skirt and jade-colored T-shirt after he silently air-spelled the word *maach,* or smooch, with his index finger on the wall to baptize our kiss, city of the same basements in which I took refuge with my and other families when Iraqi bombs were falling on Tehran, or should I say American bombs reportedly sold to both Iran and Iraq through Israel?

Never mind that I was not born there, nor that I only lived there for less than twelve years of my early life, Tehran was, is, and always will be my city, from time immemorial when stardust was cast across space to float for billions of years to coalesce into the primordial earthly larvae that left water for land to become a wandering hunter and gatherer who made stone sickles and painted cave walls to cross the grasslands of the Euphrates valley and the steppes of Central Asia to build shelter in the Bronze Age to survive the massacre of Mongols to the embryo that was conceived in the summer of love to the lemon tree and then stardust that I will become again and again, I was always evolving to be a Tehranian.

Iran seems to me now a mere place of passage, a place I crossed on my way home. To myself. I have not been able to, or rather, chosen not to, travel to Iran since 1984, the last time I left Iran. I do not foresee a change of distance between Tehran and me. Once I began Google mapping Tehran, I could not stop. Questions came flooding. Entranced, I would stay up searching until 6 a.m., then take an intoxicated dawn walk through the streets of my other city, San Francisco, coming back into my body before collapsing into another reverie.

My access to Aida Shamlou was limited. And I could not get much information from my family, tight-lipped from fear of being unkindly written about in a "memoir." But if I were to write a memoir tale-telling on my parents, I would write a book about too much love showered onto me.

Like my many selves, Tehran and I have appeared and disappeared. My mind keeps toggling between the ebbing and flowing memories. It is hard to stick to one without immediately turning toward the other.

The scent of jasmine on my bedside wafts into the frame of my awareness. It is decades since I smelled them off the long, shaded wall of my grandmother's home in Tehran, stretching obliquely into a vanishing point from one end of the narrow alley of a sleepy district. The home we visited, it seems, on a weekly basis for family lunches on Fridays. A grandmother's home is the place of treasures. A toy camel with a woolly hump and colorful tassels dangling from its ears, an abacus—perhaps a discard from my solemn patriarch grandfather's merchant warehouse where he traded tea wholesale—and other trifles buried in a tucked-away cool room that forever smelled of stillness and storage, where we cousins idled away many afternoons lost in some adventure or another, endowing these motley trinkets with magical powers, odd toys somehow gathered together in this room that we resigned ourselves to without question, worlds that transported us away from the adults and their tedious matters.

The unexpected wafts of the jasmine whose fragile stems heroically wither in a cup of water pass at random intervals through me, pleasuring the palace of hushed memories to stir something long forgotten. With each inhalation, a slice of my life imprinted on the grey matter is invoked. With each exhalation, out fades childhood one pixel at a time. Out comes a sadness whose meaning I do not know. Is it that life has so quickly passed? Is it that my grandmother is no more, and soon my father, her son, will be no more? Or that it has been so many years since I have been able to walk down that long alley in my Tehran? Or that one day no one will remember the private significance of that shaded wall in the alley? Disintegration, a destiny we are dimly aware of, uncontrollably veer toward, and eventually suffer. That jasmine is gone, long gone. Only its scent returns, spring after spring, decade after decade, and with it a reminder that all is transitory, already gone by the time we understand we cannot possibly grasp the dimension of things, just as so many stars have already burst and gone by the time we see them from our home, earth.

We hunger for significance. We impose narrative and patterns on the ongoing events of our lives. I have curated two incomplete portraits, one of myself and one of Shamlou, my *amoo*. I do not know what I would call him now if he were here. Though I bend to the giant's gravitational pull, proportions have changed, perspectives have shifted. I am no longer a wide-eyed girl. I am an adult, a creator. And so, how do I tell his story if I do not know who I am vis-à-vis him anymore?

9. SHAMLOU'S FUNERAL

ALL AT ONCE, A PANG. A flash memory explodes from a black-and-white photo that cues itself arbitrarily in my mind's eye from the carousel of my cached moments: I am climbing up my father's lean torso that is submerged in the unpainted and roughly finished rectangular watering hole in the yard of my aunt's house in Karaj, back then a village on the northwestern outskirts of Tehran at the foot of the Alborz mountains. I was around five years old wearing a terry-cloth two-piece suit.

Karaj is where the Shamlous bought their home in their later years when finances were finally allowing them a modicum of stability. According to Aida, they were leaving town, Tehran, for the weekend. By the afternoon they arrived at Karaj. They got lost trying to find the highway and drove through narrow and windy streets and crowded alleys to find themselves in a little village, different then than it is today. They were immediately enchanted, exchanging glances. Aida asks Shamlou if they had to stay in Tehran. He says, no, he works from home, they could be anywhere. Aida suggests they sell their house in Tehran and move. They agree. They buy the third house they see, the house numbered 555.[7] They chose the house for the love of a great big evergreen tree in its front yard. Fast forward to January 2000: One night, they are awakened by a deafening sound at the mute hour of 3 a.m., followed by absolute silence, total stillness in the air. The gardener rings the doorbell at 9 a.m. Aida has not peeked outside yet. She discovers that the colossal evergreen has been shattered by lightning and scattered, its branches thrown as far as their neighbors' homes. Her heart sinks. She reluctantly rolls Shamlou in his wheelchair to the window. His body was never the beneficiary of his *commitment*, she says. Shamlou senses something is wrong from her demeanor. Seeing the scene, he says, *Aysh* (endearment for Aida), *our tree is gone. I am going too. Bury me right here under this dead tree.*

Shamlou dies in Aida's arms seven months later on July 23, 2000, at the ripe hour of 9 p.m.

Uncannily, Shamlou concluded his 1960 poem, *"Genesis,"* with: *my spirit fleeting like wind and water, like rain * And a life-sucking pain like the cry of death burst in me as the old elm fell to the land by the thunder's wrath…*

During the course of *The Final Word* interview toward the end of his life, Shamlou hears about a Swedish man who wished for an excerpt of Shamlou's poem *"At the Threshold"* to be inscribed on his tombstone. When Shamlou wonders how the Swedish man found his way to the poem—was it through a translation?—the noted writer, Mahmoud Dowlatabadi, his interlocutor in this scene, says that this question needs to be asked of those who want to wipe Shamlou clean from our consciousness by removing his books from bookstores. He then quotes Shams-e Tabrizi, the poet Rumi's muse-mentor:

The world does not dare cover itself from me, nor cover me from itself.

Not one to care for his body, Shamlou suffered from various ailments throughout his life, and underwent several operations. In 1997, his right leg was amputated below the knee from gangrene caused by his diabetes, leaving him wheelchair-bound. His final relinquishing was to be inside a house numbered 555, surrounded by the sanctuary of a garden, a protective barrier for a hero whose body proved to be vincible, mortal. Aida said Shamlou reminded her of Beethoven, a majestic lion. In February 1973, when Shamlou received the Forough Farrokhzad prize in poetry, he said that he hadn't done anything yet and wished to one day deserve the honor bestowed upon him. He wished to sing his swan song.

On Thursday, July 27, Shamlou's funeral procession starts from the Iranmehr hospital in Tehran where he had received treatment. By 7 a.m., hundreds of people had already gathered on the street across from the hospital without any official announcements by the media.

The crowd is said to have steadily grown in size until a sea of people rippled down all the way to the highway at the three-way junction. The police had to close down the streets. People watch from windows, rooftops. Sunflowers and poems, cameras and photographs, wreaths and books are raised above heads. Posters and printouts of Shamlou's poetry are distributed. A large wreath dedicated from Aida reads, *"The sun of my life has set."* Other signs quote his poetry: *"The dead of this year were the most loving of the living"* (from *"Collective Love"*) and *"He who does not fear death, you lion-iron-mountain of a man, was you."* His poems are recited in unison.

At 8:30 a.m., Mahmoud Dowlatabadi, standing on the back of a pickup truck, recites a poem into a microphone that is echoed through loudspeakers. People cry. Other writers from the Writers Association of Iran, of which Shamlou was a member, recite his poems. People clap.

At 9 a.m., Mr. Dowlatabadi asks the crowd to part in order to make room for the ambulance carrying the body, which is showered with flowers as soon as it appears, moving slowly under their rain. The truck follows the ambulance. People follow peacefully, singing the national anthem, *"Ey Iran."* There are no religious chantings of *La Elaha El'Allah* (there is no God but God), the public language in a religious state, common and almost obligatory in these gatherings. A few people are selected to keep things orderly. Everyone follows the rules, a show of utmost deference by an Iranian public. Throughout, roses and gladiolas are held up high. For the majority of the procession, pens are raised above heads. There is silence, then clapping after repetitions of the national anthem. Glorious. Shamlou's recorded recitations of his own poems are broadcast. No government officials are present. It is announced that one hundred fifty buses stand ready at the three-way junction to transport attendees to the *Ememzadeh Taher* cemetery in Karaj about one hour northwest of Tehran.

By 10:45 a.m., the procession has reached the highway. The buses are filled standing room only. People continue to recite his poetry. Many drive on their own.

Outside the cemetery there are rows of parked cars and buses from other cities. It is estimated that thirty thousand people took part in the funeral. Shamlou's poems continue to be recited and broadcast at the cemetery. Mr. Dowlatabadi launches the ceremonies. Many poets and writers follow him and make speeches.

There is not enough time to relay all the messages from the sick in absentia, organizations and foundations and associations and literary groups national and abroad. Plans are made for future gatherings in honor of the poet. The poet Simin Behbahani announces, *"Shamlou never bowed to anyone or anything other than the weight of books and work."* In the end, Aida is invited to speak. She is celebrated, recognized as the one to whom contemporary Iranian literature is indebted. Ever public-shy and restrained, Aida makes a succinct remark thanking everyone for taking part in a farewell befitting the poet. More books and posters of Shamlou's likeness and poems are raised above heads. Photographs of Shamlou line candle-lit shrines. People have climbed an electric transmission tower to witness the spectacle from high up. Shamlou's physician makes a statement. The younger generations, born and raised after the revolution, crouch down at the gravesite, grim, aching, taking turns reading his poetry. One attendee notes that, overall, no one could speak in a manner truly befitting the poet, no one capable of alleviating the mourners' pain. But Shamlou's death united people, a family of humans doing their best to memorialize Shamlou. Their solidarity in numbers and intention was an act of resistance and an expression of history, bidding farewell to their poet who fought tyranny straddling two centuries.

A photo essay of the funeral shows the poet's sisters sitting against a wall. Old, somber women in black chadors, gazing downward. This could be the backyard of the Shamlou house. Another image shows a jagged top of an evergreen tree. Might this be the lightning-struck tree? In another photograph, Aida stands in dark glasses, bracing herself, enveloped in her dark scarf. One of Shamlou's sons, maybe Sirus, stands uncomfortably, awkwardly in the same frame. The two are standing apart, bodies turned away from each other, disconnected. This is the story the framing and editing of the photograph and conjecture tells. One second before, they may have been talking, or their placement in that space could have been arbitrary and not indicative of antipathy. But knowing of the tensions between Shamlou's four children and Aida, and their subsequent legal battle, which was more symbolic than constructive, it is difficult not to read the photograph that way.

Shamlou's family invites the attendees to the traditional memorial held on the seventh day from passing, on Sunday, July 30, at the house numbered 555.

I have never feared death
even if its hands are more fragile than depravity.
All my fear—in any case—is of dying in a land
where the gravedigger's pay
exceeds the worth of human freedom.[8]

Shamlou's tombstone has been vandalized and replaced many times over the years, the poet still the battlefield of a nation's conscience.

In 2016, The Ahmad Shamlou House Museum was recognized as a site of national and cultural heritage. It is treated as a site of pilgrimage by lovers of Shamlou.

Shamlou believed that poetry is the most revealing document from which a poet's social ideas could be surmised. He said his life and poetry were one and the same, inseparable.

The artist Teresita Fernández spoke of amnesia and selective memory in her 2013 commencement speech. She posed a question: If we remember by chance, why must we organize memories to mean something? Why choose one interpretation as the definitive? Why can't we offer multiple suggestions on how to read, remember, recall those pasts as readings to coexist side by side?

Although memories are fictions believed to lose fidelity with each recall, it is imperative to foray deep into the few of them that do remain with us, for they are central to the narratives constructed over time. Even the simplest ones, my memory of birthing a poem, the equivalent to Proust's taste of a madeleine unleashing a universe buried inside him, become gateways to exploration of our inner selves, our psyche, our dreams, our lives. That four-line poem is for me the big-bang moment of my genesis, whence my fictive narrative launches. At least it is for now, until another memory rises to the surface, after which the narrative is reconstructed, a whole new story is emerged until shattered by yet another new memory, or a rewriting of an existing one. I have to actively rewrite my artificial life story, to render meaningful the many heartbreaks and misadventures of my life. And to shepherd them in the service of art, of healing, not only for me, but for others.

Someone recently insisted on a neat answer to my inception. He asked whether I consider the Snow moment or my father's Question moment as the defining moment of my destiny to be an artist, or some such thing. I said that I didn't think our lives had definitive beginning points, even if we want clear demarcations for a Story. He nodded, but insisted: Did I consider one as the pivotal moment of my life? I rephrased my answer. But he insisted on a concrete answer, not my murky one. So I concede, *Yes, sure, that was the defining moment of my life.*

But you, dear reader, you know there is no beginning. You will bring your own humanity, your own potential to grasp with your sixth sense how fluid our selves are.

When I look in the mirror, I see acne scars on my cheeks, grayish-purple half-circles under my eyes, a deviated nose, sun damage, large pores, smoker's wrinkles around my mouth, a not-so-defined upper lip, a high waist, an apple of a belly, skinny inner thighs, dark and scarred knees, and I try to not turn around unless I'm striking a cha-cha pose. Occasionally, with good lighting, makeup, a certain vogue pose, I see a pleasant sight, well-executed face paint, gripping large eyes and well-arched eyebrows, the lip-glossed illusion of a fuller mouth, long, thick hair, a dignified chest, a well-calculated optical illusion achieved by pairing longer tops to balance my long legs and my short torso, and an overall elegance in my stride. All those years of dance and pilates and yoga, of watching my elegant mother walk. Sometimes, others have beheld me with kind eyes, in better light. Still others decided to turn the generosity in their eyes against me, and themselves. Seeing scars and dark circles, I was befuddled. I did not and could not imagine the source of such cruelty. They should have talked to me. We could have sat before a mirror together. I could have told them about my confusion about the circles of exclusion drawn around me, the stifled longings to belong, the years of heartache those banishments and sometimes even sabotaging and back-stabbings caused me.

Beware, if they think you're pretty, it's over. OVER.

Two months before the assassination of JFK, Shamlou writes a letter to Aida from his prison cell:

My dearest darling, it's after 4. The air is becoming milky-colored. I'm sleepy, but I can't sleep. My troubles are on my mind, and I must keep working, work that will not make us happy, nor be my prophecy, nor is this work a duty, it's for nothing, it is only to complete your Ahmad. That's why—as you say—nothing is left of Ahmad for you. But never mind these matters, one day they too shall pass. In the end, the future is ours. Yours and mine, Ahmad and Aida together.

They will finally come, nights when I will stay awake with you all night, lay your head on my chest, and tell you how happy I am next to you, how much I love you. How much I need your breath next to me! How much I have to tell you! But alas! All we have left between us is you telling me, You are tired today, *or* What a marvel that you are happy today! *or* When can I see you again? I should go, you don't get any work done when I'm here. *And I'll say,* Don't be ridiculous, you nut, stay a few more minutes! *And that's it! All the words and poems and verses that flare up inside me turn into these comical greetings that terrify me. Terrified that, little by little, you will be filled with loathing and boredom and sorrow from a love that did not find the right climate to grow in, spread its wings. I shudder at this hour of night (or shall I say, morning) from imagining such a tragedy. I stopped working to write you these few lines. My darling Aida, this bird will not sing in this cage-crypt. If you see it stifled and silent, that's why. Let it find its place, its room, so you can see how it will recite the sunniest of days in the darkest of nights. Write me so I can hear it every moment: write me so I can believe that you too are waiting for those bright nights. Write me and tell me you know this silence and degeneracy is born from life in this prison and not from us, that this is not our home, that it is not worthy of us. Write me and tell me you too await a dawn when the bird of our love will sing.*

Your Ahmad, September 20, 1963

10. THE MASTER AND MARGARITA

DURING HIS 1990–1991 VISIT, SHAMLOU TOLD ME that I reminded him of Margarita in Bulgakov's *The Master and Margarita*. I was riveted, flattered. Margarita! She immediately acquired iconic status in my mind. This is before I knew that Margarita was the full name of the diminutive Gretchen, the female character in Goethe's *Faust*, from which *The Master and Margarita* builds. I took the mention as a recommendation. But a summary of *The Master and Margarita* revealed almost nothing of Margarita, and since the synopsis didn't entice me, I did not read the book then.

Over the years, I would page through the book if I spotted a copy at a bookstore, the charge that I should read it on my mind. But continuing to find it unappealing, I would re-shelf it. This went on for two decades until I recently convinced myself that listening to its audiobook on my daily walks could be my chance to unearth the mysterious key to understanding my character as seen through the poet's eyes, as if Shamlou's likening me to Margarita were somehow a riddle, an oracle bestowed upon me until I had the readiness to receive it. And so I declared myself ready.

The novel weaves two fantastical settings, that of 1930s Moscow, where Satan appears to hold his ball, causing all manners of disarray, and of the Jerusalem of Pontius Pilate, the Roman procurator of Judea, and the Passion of Christ. Because I knew Margarita would not appear until the latter half of the book, I persisted through the complex plot, curious as to why this book was a masterpiece of the twentieth century.

Without detracting from the story-weaving gymnastics of the book and the story's intricate architecture, and what it meant for Bulgakov to write it in his time, I was otherwise frustrated that reading this book was not a transformative experience for me. I was glad to learn more about Bulgakov's life and his fraught relationship with Stalin, as well as the novel's numerous false starts since 1928, its obstacles including Bulgakov burning his manuscript—as Master famously learns in the novel that "manuscripts don't burn"—long hiatuses and several restarts, the publication of a censored version in 1966 in Russia, and finally the smuggling to Paris of the entire manuscript and publication in 1967 in its first full edition by a publisher of banned books.

Margarita is the devoted lover of Master, the novel's hero, a writer whose grief from the rejection—in a communist country—of his novel about Christ and Pontius Pilate lands him in an insane asylum. Bored in her passionless marriage, Margarita takes a leap of faith and leaves behind her old life to join Satan and his retinue. As reward for acting as the hostess of Satan's grand ball—naked, no less—and welcoming historical figures from hell, Satan grants her reunion with Master. She sets up house and a writing studio for the still-distraught Master, and in the end they are further rewarded with living a life of limbo. I felt increasingly uneasy as the story of Margarita unfolded. She was a powerless, sexualized shadow, a male fantasy, a devotee revolving around the sun of Master. Is this what Shamlou thought I was or was to become? A muse to and enabler of a male artist? Was he projecting the version of his idealized muse-assistant onto me? Was he laying the psychological groundwork for me to become a devoted planet orbiting the sun of a male artist? I tried to interpret Margarita differently, but I could not. No matter how I sliced things, this was a book by a man about a male hero in a world of male icons casting a pure and acquiescent woman as a supporting figure, reducing her to naked muse and selfless mistress.

I was reading the book at the time of 2017 #metoo and 2018 #timesup movements, which happened to coincide with my own awakening to the systematized way we women have been trivialized at the hands of male storytellers who shape a version of woman—and man, for that matter—in our imaginations, which is far from reality and stripped of our totality. I was awakening to how I had played a supporting role to my own spouse, just as Lee Krasner had done to Jackson Pollock, Alma to Gustav Mahler, women who relinquished their own lives and artistry for the expected care of their men. And as Aida had spent her life supporting the ecosystem necessary for Shamlou to meet his challenges, even if she were not giving up a creative career of her own, a potential that will never be known.

The magic spell of that characterization I safeguarded for so many years was broken: I wonder if Shamlou understood me.

We women forgo ourselves in elevating men, maintaining the *Epic of Great Men*, granting them mythic status for imposing their version of the world onto us, reflecting a set of the realities we adopt as truth. In the meantime, we are ignored, used as tools, unaware of the history of our own exploitation because it has become so deeply embedded that we too see ourselves by those narratives, complicit in perpetuating that male world order.

This is how my discomfort in the world multiplied as I grew up. If I spoke up, I felt a kind of tension arise from others, men, which I internalized. Eyes would roll or gloss over, a hand would dart at me under or at table and eye level, gestures of silencing and disdain, sometimes obliging me with a few precious moments to speak. And then there was the other extreme, of too much interest for being categorized as *other, an exotic woman,* equally as limiting and demoralizing.

A friend suggests there might exist a slim chance that Shamlou likening me to Margarita did not stem from his projecting a male gaze onto me, but as an augur of a possibility that I might allow my own surrender rather than insist on my own art. I can't be sure about whether Shamlou saw a compliant woman in me, with abundant and romantic enthusiasm to idolize men, which he wanted to forewarn me of and challenge. But any interpretation of his comment is guesswork at this point. My friend asks whether I asked Shamlou *why* I reminded him of Margarita. I do not remember whether I did, nor do I remember thinking this was important at the time. I just assumed that he saw through me with laser eyes, that his word was sacred. *Why* did I not ask? *Did* I not ask? My friend says she is sure he cared for me the artist, plenty clear from his bothering to visit.

As such, I rebel against the role I have played into. I retroactively reclaim years of energies spent to perform at my peak muse for the boyfriends who identified me as one, who drained my passions, intuition, sexuality, intelligence, and emotional exuberance, SUCKING MY BLOOD for their personal purposes. I saw myself through their eyes, not because I lacked a kernel of creativity, but because this was the only way they could relate to me, so that seemed the only way to connect with them. I was fully capable of what they were attempting—and then some. Ah, youth! You were soft.

I take back all that passion. Lady M. rallied the might for that reclaiming best:

"…Come you spirits
That tend on mortal thoughts, unsex me here,
And fill me from the crown to the toe top-full
Of direst cruelty! make thick my blood;
Stop up the access and passage to remorse,
That no compunctious visitings of nature
Shake my fell purpose, nor keep peace between
The effect and it! Come to my woman's breasts,
And take my milk for gall, you murd'ring ministers,
Wherever in your sightless substances
You wait on nature's mischief! Come, thick night,
And pall thee in the dunnest smoke of hell,
That my keen knife see not the wound it makes,
Nor heaven peep through the blanket of the dark,
To cry "Hold, hold!"[9]

I recently managed to argue with and alienate two old, white men of some power and status within twenty minutes of arrival at one of the men's event, men who were too entitled to remotely consider listening to my point of view. Instead they exerted unquestionable dominance, lectured to put me in my place after I questioned their assumptions. As usual, I let their little egos jousting for their place to have the last word in order to save the social situation, because I was someone's guest, so it reflected on him—I had to save his ego, too. At least this time I did not bat an eyelash about talking back to the men for fear that I might lose an opportunity only these old men could dangle over my head and in the end not provide. I decided they would never have anything to offer me to merit my complicity in their game. And I did not need their permission. Those days and that Good Girl are gone.

I was a precocious child, interrupted by social expectations of compliance, treated as a wide-eyed ingenue for most of my adult life by men who have *shoulded* me, mistaking my voracity in asking questions while making up my own mind for an invitation to *tell me what to do*. When in fact, I have been deciding my own fate all along, only I've been a late bloomer in asserting that fact to the world.

Sometimes I am so amped up about feeling spurned that I curse the rug not anchored by a sticky mat gathering under the cramped wooden chair I keep rearranging to escape my anxiety. My domestic shortcomings just enrage me more. The damned fidgeting. The damned body. Where else can I vent these grievances but here on this page by the utter force of my own conviction to be brutally honest?

The rage wells up, bottomless, replenishing. Rage that explodes onto the world but is directed at myself, prompts me to repel, alienates me from my fellow humans. The rage rears its head, a panic that springs up at trivial concerns—not being able to tuck a piece of paper into a bag and the impending paper cut, a sudden sound that disturbs the moat of silence and isolation I have crafted around myself against the world. I wish I could attribute it to the frustrations of *being a spiritual being having a physical experience. La Dee Da.* But alas, I cannot. The enlightened spiritual being is only a reverie. I am light years away from pure spirit, tainted by my earthly existence and tendings to the business of living. Was this rage embedded in my DNA? Primal yelps of my ancestors—my raped foremothers, my massacred forefathers, my hunted people—persisting across time through my vessel? Or did I learn it from watching those around me having their turns at their own rage? Inherited either way, my rage deprives me of the pleasures of my entitled flesh, drives me to deny myself happiness. And yet, my animal body greedily grasps to shape each moment into its best. And yet again, how impossible to sustain this when pain—physical, emotional, self-inflicted or not—intervenes.

But rage is only the flip side of the coin of grief.

Outside, the mid-afternoon lull of my city. The electric saw of construction work, a motorcycle whirring in the distance, a chirp here and there, the distant hum of traffic, the edge of my curtain billowing from the breeze through the cracked window, the sweet California air, the silhouette of Mount Tamalpais in the distance against the wide blue sky. It is 3:42 p.m., the hour in which hope pulsates. Now is the hour I must steal away to confront the world, or rather, escape my self-imposed isolation, belong somewhere in the family of other drifters. Any later than this, I will keep staying home and descending more into isolation. Twilight comes. Still the hour of promise. Of a day well-stretched, and of a night of potentials. I write to get under the surface of things.

EMERGENCE

The herald
of flocking birds ricochets from all corners
of the sky. I receive
like an antenna, humbled by their dimension
head craned in
the meager window to capture

                            their expanding

shape as I lock
myself in a room

                   hurl

myself at the walls crouching down to conjure.
Little limited me.
Bursting into the sky
as they do,
honest, the arrowhead of them,
instinct piloting their whirring wings,
they dive and soar every which way.
How I want
to thrust
myself into every speck of sky.
The gravelly road crunches
The trees that cycle through
spells sit brittle and fawny,
tilt into winter then spring without
inquest holding
their place in the scheme
of things.

Dream of 2001 When Performing 8 Shows per Week

Two nights before the last time I danced on stage

On top of the theater's glass geodesic dome two figures
teeter, shadows of myself.
I stop in the middle of my dance routine and point
up to them from stage, molasses-slow.
The audience gazes up
in darkness. I see friends.
The theater is burning.
Masses flood down the grand staircase

I run for a long time through night streets
I open my door and run a straight line to the back door

which I open onto my small enclosed backyard to
find its walls, ground, and sky covered flush

with blazing
autumn leaves—corals, and reds, and golds.
A pearly white torso of Venus de Milo sits
on a black pedestal, blood branching down her chest.
My upstairs neighbor appears
on the back staircase, points to Venus:

Congratulations! You are dead!
smiling big at me with eerily open eyes.

The most important lesson my mother taught me was while we were being cruel to each other in my car. I was drifting. My mother said:

Go where you can make the most contribution. Dance was never going to be it.

Parents risk alienating their own flesh by uttering the harshest truths over and over. I threw a tantrum about her blindness to dance as art form, blah blah blah, dropped her off at a remote strip mall, drove away. She had to call my father who would pick her up while I was en route home. When I drove away, I felt the distance between me and my mother, between the daughter who would never do that and me. To leave your mother somewhere alone in the night.

She was right of course. All my art had sat inside me without a real conduit, without a mastered craft. I had been trying to express through limited means, like a color film playing on a black-and-white television. My mother liberated my art.

I think about translation, and miscommunication. The distorted language we deploy on each other, an engine veering off its intended track, like twisted hips that catapult a gymnast into a reckless direction. Whole courses are launched, paths carved, enmities cast from language incomplete, fragmentary, retranslated, decontextualized, misinterpreted or, heartbreakingly, misused.

12. THE BIRTH OF A TRANSLATOR

"The role of the artist is exactly the same as the role of the lover. If I love you, I have to make you conscious of the things you don't see."

— James Baldwin

A T FIRST I BRUSHED OFF A FRIEND'S SUGGESTION. Her life had recently been enriched, Sally said, collaborating as the English-language native speaker with a newly arrived immigrant Uzbek woman to bring the poetry of the Uzbek poet, Dilshad, into English, and she wanted the pleasure of that indulgence with me. But despite the fact of having heard Shamlou discuss his translation of *The Little Prince* among other works, of having read the Western Canon in the Persian language (also known as Farsi, its endonym) first and then in English, and of having studied Comparative Literature, translations of the *Iliad* and the *Odyssey* and *Don Quixote* and so many others chosen for me by my instructors, whose translators' names were largely omitted from book credits by the publishers' design to gloss over the "foreignness" of these works, as well as attending seminars by Jacques Derrida who lectured in multiple languages, I had never given translation a second thought. I never thought some lonely literary intermediary toiled to grant me access to whole new worlds. The irony.

The translator is only visible when she has failed, when the reader wants to throw a book at the wall.

This invisibility was the station of translation within the literary discourse in the United States not two decades ago. Since then, minors, majors, and Ph.D.s in literary translation are offered at universities, new literary journals and publishers have cropped up devoted solely to literature in translation, existing literary journals and publishers have upped their number of international works in translation, and new awards and grants are available for the making and publishing of translated literature. So while we are woefully behind other countries in access to international literature, to the tune of 3 percent here versus upwards to 35 percent elsewhere—because the Empire wouldn't be the Empire if it didn't propagate its own narrative and exclude that of others—we are a little bit better off than we were two decades ago.

Of course, I did not know that I was about to live through a translation renaissance of sorts. But my friend persisted, her pining chronicles of poetic imagery from a new world that had intoxicated her as we stood at the ballet barre doing our *tendus* and *pliés* gradually tempted me.

So I succumbed. There was nothing to lose. Sally was a gentle soul, a lady of grace, so spending this kind of time with her braided yet another thread into our burgeoning friendship. And I was in a transitional moment, that pregnant lull that invites myriad new adventures.

And so began a new life, illuminated already in the choosing of what to translate, the journey into the literature of my mother tongue, treasure troves of the distant and yet familiar bound in old, frayed editions that traveled thousands of miles across an ocean to wait stacked in moving boxes, then passed on from parent to child, passaged city to city to sit silently on bookshelves. A new life ignited even in the summoning of all the Persian language that had lain dormant in me, in the effort and the reaching out to more experienced readers to understand three pages of poetry, word by word, line by line, idea by idea, image by image, reference by reference, only to encounter the real task at hand, the infinite possibility of interpretation, and then the delicate labor of the poem's pilgrimage from the original into the new, target language. In rendering that one poem lay the birth of all the questions a translator would ever ask of herself as she realized the responsibility of the work, the epiphany that each of the thousand choices to be made danced the poem into wildly distinct living, breathing creatures, and that those selections made the difference between a superior or an amateur, or lexically faithful yet drab or loyal yet innovative poem in the new language. The questions of how much of the original culture to leave in—what I later learned was a practice of "foreignization" in translation theory—and how much to assimilate it to the new culture, or "domestication," and how easily a literature becomes colonized in extreme practices of domestication.

Suddenly, there was an outlet, a magical gateway into my inner worlds whose bridging had not yet discovered expression. A scaffolding for wordsmithing, verbal creativity, solving linguistic puzzles, for pulling from the universe to render a word or a line, for exercising the left and the right brains. For combining math and craft with art and alchemy. This unavoidable practice of personal, cultural, temporal, spatial, and linguistic translation that had consumed immigrant-me on every level, the negotiations of the self vis-à-vis both sides, now had utility.

I. FELL. IN. LOVE.

More and more, the translator's invisibility began to dawn on me. For example, Milan Kundera's book, *The Unbearable Lightness of Being*, came to the forefront of popular consciousness after Philip Kaufman's 1988 film of the successful book. But does anyone know the name of the book's distinguished and prolific translator, Michael Henry Heim? Heim was also the translator of Thomas Mann's *Death in Venice*, of Kundera's *The Book of Laughter and Forgetting*. Or does the public take note of whose translation of *Crime and Punishment* or Neruda or Rumi they are reading? The invisibility of a translator was part of the reality of the book market, but does not have to be.

A few years after this discovery, and before realizing the magnitude of Heim's legacy myself, I would get to spend an afternoon with Heim and his wife, Priscilla, at their home not far from UCLA where he taught. I was brought over to his house and introduced by a former student of his as a young translator with a multidisciplinary approach to my work. Heim and his wife sat engrossed for one whole hour to watch the video footage of *ICARUS/RISE*, the theatrical project I had created in which I dramatized fourteen poems from the anthology I would later finish editing and translating, *Belonging: New Poetry by Iranians Around the World*, as a musical-visual work. It was a most uncomfortable hour for me, squirming through a video capture of a live performance I was giving with other artists. Heim was so present, so encouraging. He introduced my work to people at PEN American Center who applied for a New York State Council on the Arts translation grant for me, the third translation award I would receive.

The poem I chose to translate with Sally was *"Tavallodi Digar,"* which we translated into *"Another Birth,"* the title poem of a book by the daring Iranian poet Forough Farrokhzad (1934–1967) who, in battling the patriarchal fabric of society and the intelligentsia in the mid-twentieth century, reimagined the language of poetry in general, including of poetry by women.

It was on those still afternoons as I sat with Sally on my red futon under the kitchen window that showered it with sunlight, where we wept, each defending our choices, why "pond," not "pool," that I fell in love. I fell in love with the joyous hours of research, the probing into endless fields, the dreaming, the analogue-findings, the bond this pastime was making between the poet Farrokhzad, me, the poet Partow Nooriala who was helping me read the poem, Sally, the new poem in English, and eventually its new readers. I was a link in that lineage of love.

This love carried me through *Belonging: New Poetry by Iranians Around the World*, which took five years to edit and translate. The idea was to show that Iran had a much wider and more recent poetic tradition than Rumi, the thirteenth century Persian poet readers of English know from the abundance of his work in translation, not to mention the "new-age-ifications" of his work saturating the market and popular culture.

My hunger for knowledge led me to conferences populated by other like-minded writer-translators who discovered literary worlds they wanted to share. In the process, I awakened to the marginality of translating a culture that suffers from brutal sanctions, one that not only offers no support to its writers and artists through advocacy, international exchanges, grants and opportunities, but in fact, persecutes and murders its artists.

Iran is not a signatory of the Berne Convention for the Protection of Literary and Artistic Works and does not have a bilateral relationship with the United States. Iranian publishers translate and publish books from other countries without extending royalties. Therefore, little are the incentives for those publishers, particularly those whose books are being black-marketed in Iran, to obtain rights, commission translations, and publish Iranian literature produced in Iran.

For the most part, because of Iran's refusal to become a signatory of the Berne Convention, works first produced in Iran are considered in the public domain, and its translators are often free to translate those texts from the Persian. Most translators want to have rights anyway, for ethical reasons, and because most publishers ask for rights. All in all, the copyright landscape is murky legal grounds, a no man's land for translators from the Persian. Without standardized and well-defined protocol, with decades of sanctions marring international relations between Iran and the United States, translators often launch from uncertain grounds.

This shifts the publishing balance in favor of literatures from countries that play nice with each other, countries that are not vilified. Translations constitute a small percentage of books published in the United States, somewhere between 0.3 and 3 percent. Literary translations are especially on the fringes. But literature translated from the Persian and published in the U.S. market stands on the fringes of the fringes. This explains the stark contrast between the availability of Iranian literature in translation versus the primacy and visibility of English translations of German, French, Italian, Spanish, even Arabic and Chinese literatures, supported through cultural institutions, awards, and mentorship programs.

Iranian literature also suffers from curation for narratives of pain and politics rather than aesthetics and innovations. Some advocates of Iranian literature self-exotify, not realizing that they fuel this curation, or perhaps they turn a blind eye in favor of lucrative careers catering to othering agendas reinforced by best-selling books like *Reading Lolita in Tehran* and its not-so-subtle message that brown women were saved by Henry James and Vladimir Nabokov, and not by their own thousand years of literary history.

These profiteers of crisis are emboldened since few question them. Lack of widespread access to Iran allows them to spread misinformation, skew the perspective. Even the most left-leaning liberals of the West unknowingly lap up these othered narratives that keep alive the Empire.

The academic patriarchy, guardians of imaginary and unfortunate gates, envisioning themselves to be the sole arbiters of all things *Persianate*, have been of limited help. Decades ago, before new generations of near-native English-speaking translators grew up to tackle the work of bridging Iranian literature to the Anglophone reader, they produced academic translations of the Iranian canon in their scholarly English, books that did not reach the greater public, but inform intermediaries to the mass market. When I began sharing my translations, some academics felt their fiefdoms infringed upon by a non-academic female who had not climbed their hierarchies of apprenticeship begging for permission to continue *their* work. One such academic, an old Iranian man, derided my work just after my presentation during a panel discussion we both took part in, later refused me any endorsement, and shook his patriarchal index finger in my face chiding me for the audacity to unearth new poets *he* had not found or sanctioned me to translate, punishing me as if I were an unruly child.

But I give these men too much credit for cornering the market on exclusion. Some female Iranian academics have done the same. I recently found an email I sent to directors of a new Iranian studies program curating a conference of Iranians in diaspora. I wrote to introduce my work (they knew of it) and to list all the different "novelists, poets, bloggers, editors, journalists, website editors, translators, nonfiction writers, and multimedia artists" they had invited to present at their conference, further proposing, "As an Iranian-American artist living in California and creating collaborative projects around Iranian diaspora literature, I would love to be involved. I see that you have recently added two participants. Perhaps you can add one more to make your event even more 'representative' for your audience?" No response, and two decades later, still no invitation.

This kind of omission started back then and has continued for the most part to the present. Yet, not all academics have dismissed me. For each "gatekeeper" there have been several generous, open-minded collaborators who understand that our work is complementary.

And then there are those whose dismissal hinges upon the assumption that anything but perfect fluency in the source language is an automatic disqualification to translate. They confuse their discomfort in reading creative translations that are not word for word for a translator's unfamiliarity with and disloyalty to the source language, and likely do not realize that the translator's task is access to the source language and mastery in rendering it into the target language, not vice versa. Access to the source language can be achieved even without fluency in it, through work with intermediaries making trots, with living authors when possible, reference books, and collaborators with different linguistic skills—how Shamlou practiced translation. To me, translation is always some form of teamwork. The moment we open a dictionary or thesaurus, collaboration has commenced.

Translators from the Persian float like islands at conferences in the midst of a sea of translators who are to varying degrees in better positions than we are. We find ourselves in petty turf wars, orphans without a literary axis to turn on. How are we to ever catch up, even rise, against these hurdles? Translation and its obstacles, the battleground of othered literature, became my preoccupation.

I step into the bathtub. For a few seconds the world is right. Suddenly, my body hydroplanes on what seems like an oily surface and I am surfing involuntarily toward the drain in slow motion. In an instant I find myself in the utterly disorienting position of almost-toppled-over with one leg up in the air. Time slows down. In these circumstances we are so undeniably present that we feel every nanosecond of it, which warps our senses and makes time seem much fuller. At this point my only goal is to gauge where and in which position I am falling, so that I can approximate the right place to direct an extended arm and cushion myself. I owe this to being a regular teeterer on and maneuverer of high heels out and about, and on the dance floor in sweeping forward, side, and back jumps of fancy. I land hard on the palm of a hand whose pinky finger had recently broken and not exactly healed, curved and pointing perpetually upward like a wayward talon on the side of my hand. My pinky had folded back onto itself like a dial on a speedometer, like the crescent arc of the sun across in the sky, like a butterfly-open book closing, from the force of friends tackling me with love-hugs in their home, where I was sleeping on their couch awaiting their return. For a moment I think that I have yet again damaged my fingers in an absurd event. But despite the white palm from landing on my right hand, its fingers seem fine.

13. A SKYROCKETING, 2003–2013

THE UNIVERSE UNLOCKED BY TRANSLATION and a blind spot to limitations of the body, resources, and time, and the inexhaustible decade of my thirties all coincided.

In 2003, I began an MFA program to study nonfiction, and swapped into poetry for one semester, all the while editing and translating my first book, the anthology *Belonging*. That, and my résumé of performance projects, garnered me a substantial arts grant that came with the grantors' condition that I create multimedia works inspired by the poetry I was translating. I found myself launching a nonprofit organization around this unexpected creative direction without any prior knowledge as to what it would mean and how to manage one. From there unfolded poetry-videos, theatrical and collaborative performances of the poems, festivals, and a mini-movement of sorts under the auspices of the nonprofit.

In hours, I have wasted at least two to three years of my life thus far writing one proposal after another. Fundraising. I have won some and lost many, but what would have happened if I had only taken the commission-me-and-I'll-make-art path? If and when they asked, it was mostly to make work as a *woman of color*. So, instead, I bet on myself and the art I wanted to make. If I translate Iran, it's because *I* want to do it, not because *you* expect me to. I curse my independence, entre-preneurial spirit, intractable vision, and ability to organize.

Grant proposals force artists to discuss, declare, insist on, and showcase their IDENTITY. I never *felt* any of the things I had to classify myself as. The identity politics of being a female, immigrant, Iranian-American artist bypassed me. That's for *others*, for *their* practice of equity. I have brown eyes, but I don't *feel* it. I know others will roll their eyes

—my

self

my

real

self is

curious monkey. That's all.

There is cumulative wisdom in life, but I am a child, I throw myself into the unknown. My explorer's innocence serves as a platform for those wrapped up in definitions and certainty to put on airs, treat it with disdain—*Shouldn't she know what she is doing? Who the hell does she think she is? Why?* That's OK, I have learned. *Why?* THE WORK SHOWS YOU HOW TO DO IT. *Why?* Because I want to KNOW. That's why.

Following my work, I began to conceive and write the libretto—the sung text—for classical musical works, culling from and remixing characters and ideas from Persian mythology and folklore and poetry. All the things I did not know and was dying to.

14. MY SHAMLOU PROJECTS

ON **DECEMBER 12, 2012, THE 87TH ANNIVERSARY** of Shamlou's birth, I waited until midnight and cold-called Aida Shamlou 11.5 hours ahead at her home in Karaj. I awkwardly addressed her as Auntie Aida, even so many years later. She remembered me and said I sounded the same as I had so many years ago. She sounded emotional. I held back tears in several moments of silence before I was able to utter these words: *I called on the birthday of the great poet to say I want to create a book and an opera inspired by him.*

The book I imagined would be a "Shamlou Reader," selections of the poet's work in translation. The opera would be conceived and its libretto written by me. Libretto, from the Italian, is the diminutive of the word *libro,* meaning book.

At the time of my call to Mrs. Shamlou, I had worked as a librettist on one song cycle for a classical music piece, *Fire Angels,* a piece commemorating the tenth anniversary of September 11, 2001, that had its world premiere at Carnegie Hall. I had happened upon the expression through my work translating Persian poetry, which led a composer to invite me to create a piece possibly inspired by Persian poetry, which was ultimately an original invention inspired by Indo-Iranian mythological and philosophical concepts.

But I had never created an opera, and had no prospects of a commission. One year after the phone call to Aida, I had been accepted to join an opera residency program as a librettist. For my first assignment in 2014, a *recitative* (dialogue) scene, I sketched an imaginary scene between Aida and one of Shamlou's adult children, who appears unexpectedly at the door of the Karaj home to haul away the worldly belongings of the poet. I had read about the legal battles over Shamlou's will in the year since I first contacted Aida, about Shamlou's adult children feeling entitled to the tangible belongings of Shamlou's estate as a kind of blood compensation, while the management of Shamlou's works—the more meaningful portion of his estate—had been bequeathed mainly to Aida Shamlou and another person I will call Mr. X. One of Shamlou's sons (now deceased) representing the siblings, won the court case and auctioned off furniture for a small sum, the loss of minor tangibles a tragic turn of events, as they could have furnished the future Shamlou House Museum.

Shamlou appeared again in *The Investment*, a short opera I wrote in 2015 for another opera residency. This time I named the protagonist after an early, long poem of his, *"Roxana,"* the invocation of an unattainable fantasy. My story was about Roxana, a young Iranian-American painter who stands up for herself and her art when the new-Silicon-Valley-money collector of her painting—which he discovers during the scene is inspired by Roxana's mother's favorite poet from the old country, Ahmad Shamlou—attacks Roxana for giving credence to a controversial figure, a man he accuses of betraying Iran with his *Shahnameh* commentary.

But in both these instances, the absence of prior context on this cultural figure and the struggle to embed some context within a story's exposition was a creative hurdle, what seemed to always be a challenge in my projects, working from a culture whose figures and folktales and myths are unknown to another—the fetishized and Orientalized Alibaba, Sheherazad, and the like notwithstanding. And it was not encouraging to be offered a second opera by the producer of the first residency, only with one caveat: not to write an opera with Iranian characters or about Iran, so as "not to let the emotional involvement get in the way of your craft." My final assignment with this producer, a short opera, had been more or less the opening scene of *Superman*, a universal story of parents agonizing about sending their children away when their home country is in ruins, but set in 1983 Iran during the devastating war with Iraq. Would I be given that caveat if I were writing the same story with Italian names? I doubt an American librettist of European descent would be told not to write American characters because of "emotional involvement." It felt a lot like xenophobia. The project of erasing the narratives of people from *patria non grata* is so ingrained, so normalized, it is nearly invisible.

Nevertheless, I had heard myself utter grandiose aspirations before, some of which eventually became completed projects, so I was in for a Shamlou opera, whatever the challenges and costs.

And there would be many.

Soon after the call to Karaj, I launched a serious study of Shamlou's vast body of work, putting together a dossier of fragments from Aida's anecdotes about their love and beginnings and other material I would read and view. I translated excerpts of Shamlou's poetry and pasted them into the text that I was writing inspired by his poetic imagery and personal life. The dossier grew in volume, becoming what I like to call a "soup" in all of my projects, where all the information gathers, simmers, dissolves, and reintegrates. I began extracting sections to make a libretto draft, a series of songs around the enduring love of Aida and Shamlou, and the idea of home and the lack thereof in the uncertain and nomadic life the Shamlous lived both from the lack of means and from living abroad on and off.

At one point the opera was loosely structured as composer Osvaldo Golijov and librettist David Henry Hwang's *Ainadamar, an Opera in Three Images,* the story of poet and playwright Federico García Lorca and his lover and muse, Catalan actress Margarita Xirgu, told in a series of reverse flashbacks. Shamlou felt kinship with Lorca, both poets filled with zeal for their social ideas, symbols of freedom. Shamlou translated *Blood Wedding,* among other works of Lorca.

In early 2014, I received permission from Mrs. Shamlou to translate and publish Shamlou's work.

I submitted my translations to a prestigious U.S. fellowship, and won my fifth translation award for my translations of Ahmad Shamlou's poetry in August 2014. Not in my wildest dreams would I have imagined how my life would be turned upside down in October 2014.

15. POEMS BY AHMAD SHAMLOU

"I feel kinship with human beings who do not hide daggers up their sleeve, whose brows are not furrowed, nor their smiles a ruse with which to violate other people's rights and shelter. I neither prefer Iranian over non-Iranian, nor Iranian over Iranian. I am a Persian-speaking Turk Lori Baluchi Persian Kurd, an African European Australian American Asian, a brown-skinned yellow-skinned red-skinned white who not only has no problems with himself, but also none with others. Rather, I feel the terror of death under my skin without the company of others. I am a human being among other humans on this sacred planet earth, meaningless without their presence. I prefer poetry to be a blaring trumpet rather than a lullaby."

— Ahmad Shamlou

COLLECTIVE LOVE

Tears are a mystery
Smiles a mystery
Love a mystery
The tears of that night were the smile of my love.
I am not a tale to be told
Not a song to be sung
Not a sound to be heard
Or something that you can see
Or something that you can know
I am Common Pain
Cry me out!

The tree speaks with the woods
The weed with the fields
The star with the galaxy
And I speak with you
Tell me your name
Give me your hand
Speak me your words
Give me your heart
I have discovered your depths
And spoken for all through your lips
And your hands are familiar with mine.

I have wept in blazing solitude with you
For the sake of the living
And have sung the most beautiful of songs

In the darkest of graveyards
For the dead of this year
Were the most loving of the living.

Give me your hand
Your hands know me
Oh you found-at-last, I speak with you
As the cloud with the storm
The weed with the fields
The rain with the sea
The bird with spring
And the tree that speaks with the woods
For I have discovered your depths
For my voice is
Intimate with yours.

(From *Fresh Air*, 1955)

THE BEGINNING

Out of nowhere
in an unknown land
as time was ripening—

this is how I was born
in a thicket of sticks and stones
and my heart
began to beat
in the void.

———

I left the cradle of repetitions
in a birdless land without spring.

My first journey was a return
from the dispiriting sights of sand and spikes,
not having traveled far with my first, untaught, newborn steps.

My first journey
was a return.

———

The far distance
offered no hope.
Faltering
on brand-new legs
            I stood facing the dazzling horizon.

I discovered that there was no promise
for a mirage stood in the way.

—◦◦◦—

The far distance offered no hope.
I learned that there was no promise:
This endlessness

      was a prison so colossal

                that the spirit

hid
behind tears
      ashamed of ineptitude.

(From *Aida in the Mirror*, March 1961)

GENESIS

There was the faint breath of wind and the thin silk of moonlight and fountain and garden * And it was on the fourth midnight when the new bride landed from home in the moonstruck garden wandering * pondering the new heat coursing through her breasts' blue veins * itself like the earth's burning fever that feeds unripe lemons * And there was in her eyes that watched the moonlight and flora shame from the newly awakened lust burning in her loins * unquenchable itself like the ever-insatiable thirst of grass—means to the meadow's greenness * And she was shameful of a long-awaited faltering and fleeting memory of what befell her body, between her—alien to the event—and a fierce alien-man swift and wise with the ways of her body * sweeping so covetous a hand on her sleeping body * moving as a breeze charged with the scent of sunsoaked grass that peels away the blossom-sheaths to reveal the unripe seed.

There was the faint breath of wind and the thin silk of moonlight * and the garden's fountain that danced in the little pond with its swaying lithe arms * And on the fourth midnight the new bride slumbered on the stretch of grass * And in the same breath, I was in the newly sprouted leaves * or in the fluttering breeze * and perhaps even in the deep waters * And the breath of the wind stirring little blossoms on the thick tree wailed in me * and bright streams of rain wept in me. *

There was the faint breath of wind and the thin silk of moonlight and the garden's fountain * And on the fourth midnight the new bride sleeping on the bed of newly sprouted grass with fire in her core trembled unto herself from sensing a man beside her * And I was neither leaf nor lake * nor wind or rain * Oh you Plant Spirit! My body was your prison house * And the new bride was inseminated by the spirit of tree and wind and water before sensing my father's lips upon hers on the fourth midnight * And I turned a leafless and windless city into my prison house without the memory of wind and leaf ever escaping me.

My eyes were like two elm leaves when I was born, my veins like waterlily vine, my hands maple claws * my spirit fleeting like wind and water, like rain * And a life-sucking pain like the cry of death burst in me as the old elm fell to the land by the thunder's wrath *

And I was, oh you strife-stained nature, oh father! your child.

(From *Instants and Eternity*, 1960)

NOCTURNE[10]

And he who heard the truth was not heard from again.

— Saadi

And he who knew

        held his tongue

and he would spoke

        did not know…

—⁓—

What a night of sorrows it was!
And the traveler passing through that silent dark
provoking dogs by the sound of his horse hooves on stone
without pondering even for one second
to dismount for the night

        all seemed

like a fever dream.

What a night of sorrows it was!

(From *Instants and Eternity*, November 1961)

RIVER

To relinquish oneself to the bedrock of destiny
and to reveal a secret of discontent
with every pebble.

How sweet is the river's murmur!

—~~—

To plummet from the spike of one's pride
And to plunge from the noble pure-heartedness of isolation
Crying from the terror of each fall.

How glorious is the thunder of waterfalls!

—~~—

And to keep plunging down the rift's grade
and to rise to battle
with every boulder.

What an epic the river is, what an epic!

(From *Phoenix in the Rain*, January 25, 1966)

POVERTY

I am weary of anguish that is not mine
I inhabit an earth that is not mine
I live with a name that is not mine
I weep from pain that is not mine
I stir from joy that is not mine
I will die a death that is not mine.

(From *The Garden of Mirrors*, 1959)

FAREWELL

To exist, two hearts are needed—
one heart to love, one heart to be loved
one heart to gift, one heart to receive
one heart to speak, one heart to respond
one heart for me, one heart for the one I desire
to feel a human by my side.

—◁◇▷—

The seas in your eye can be dried up
I want a fertile wellspring.
Your breasts are little stars
Behind the stars, I want a human:

a human who chooses me
a human I choose
a human who looks at my hands
a human whose hands I can look at
a human by my side
to look at the hands of humans together
a human by my side, a mirror by my side
to laugh in, to cry in…

—◁◇▷—

The gods were not saving me
and your brittle union
did not save me either

Not your brittle union

      not the eyes and not your breasts

                    not your hands

your heart was not a mirror by my side

your heart had no humanity by my side…

(From *Fresh Air*, 1955)

UNFINISHED GHAZAL...

To each strand of my soul, a hundred songs
Alas that there is no hand at the pick.
Like a dream, I lived in longing, for night
faded and no one desired to share the night with me.

(From *Instants and Eternity,* 1960*)*

SONG OF ACQUAINTANCE

Who are you that I
so trustingly
confide my name to
hand the keys of my home to
share the bread of my joy with
sit by whose side
at whose knees
and so peacefully
sleep?

Who are you that I
so solemnly linger
with in the country
of my dreams?

(From *Aida in the Mirror*, May 19, 1963)

YOU AND I...

You and I are one single mouth
singing in all its singsong
a more beautiful ballad.

You and I are one single sight
renewing the world
                    each instant
                           in its view.

We hate
whatever hinders us
whatever limits us
whatever forces us
                    to look to the past—

a hand
that sweeps an insolent line in vain.

———~~~———

You and I are one single fever
greater than any flame
defeat will never conquer us
for we are invincible-bodied
by this love.

———~~~———

And a dove nesting under our shelter

floods the house to the brim

in its hasty fluttering

            with a forgotten

                    god.

(From *Aida in the Mirror*, January 13, 1963)

AIDA IN THE MIRROR

Your lips
        tender as a poem
transform the most lustful kisses into such innocence
that the cave-dwelling creature reaps
their rewards to become human.
And your cheeks
           with two oblique grooves
that guide your pride and
               my fate,
I who have endured the night
               unarmed
awaiting morning,
and collected
a noble maidenhood sealed
from the brothels of commerce.

Never did anyone so ruinously rise to suicide that I settled into life!

—⁓—

And your eyes are the secret of fire.

And your love the victory of humankind
when it rushes to the battle of fate.

And your embrace
A little retreat to live in
A little retreat to die in

An escape from the city

        that brazenly accuses

                the sky's purity

with a thousand fingers.

—⁓—

Mountains come into being with the first rocks
and humans with the first pain.

In me lived a cruel prisoner
unable to adapt to the song of his chains—
I came into being with your first gaze.

—⁓—

Tempests

      play a reed

          gloriously

              in your grand dance,

and the song of your veins
makes rise the eternal sun.

Let me awake from slumber with such might
that city streets
will seek my company.

Your hands are reconciliation,
companions that help banish
enmity

      from

          memory.

Your brow is a towering mirror
radiant and towering
into which the Seven Sisters gaze
to behold their beauty.

Two restless birds sing inside your breast.
From where will summer arrive
for thirst
to make all the waters more quenchable?

I searched for a lifetime in the mirror
until you appeared in it.
I cried pools and oceans,
oh you fairy-like in human mold
whose body burns only in the firepit of falsehood!
Your presence is a heaven
that justifies escape from hell
an ocean that engulfs me
to wash me clean
of all sins and lies.

And dawn awakes by your hands.

(From *Aida in the Mirror,* January 1964)

NOCTURNE

If it is beautiful in vain, night,
then why is it beautiful,
                    night
for whom is it beautiful?—

Night
       and its unelliptical river of stars
that run a cold path.
And reliving which memory
       with the breathtaking ode of toads
do long-haired mourners
on both banks of the river
                    lament
when each dawn
is pierced
with a chorus
of twelve shots?

If it is beautiful in vain, night,
then why is it beautiful, night
for whom is it beautiful?

(From *Abraham in Flames*, March 16, 1972)

ON THE WINTER WITHIN

All
    of the trembling of my hands and heart
                          was for
love
      to become a refuge

not a flight,
but a sanctuary.

Oh love, oh love
Your blue face is not visible.

—————

And the cool of a salve
               on the flame of a wound
not the fury of a flame
on the winter within.

Oh love, oh love
Your red face is not visible.

—————

The dark dust of solace
        on the presence of frailty
and the den of deliverance
            on the flight of presence,
darkness
      on the calm of blue
and the green of a little leaf
          over the purple bloom.

Oh love, oh love
Your familiar color
is not visible.

(From *Abraham in Flames,* 1973)

THE ONE WHO SAYS I LOVE YOU

The one who says I love you
is a sad balladeer
who has lost his song.

If only love
were the language of words

There are a thousand joyous
                songbirds in your eyes
A thousand silent canaries in my throat.

If only love
were the language of words

The one who says I love you
is the grief-stricken heart of a night
seeking its moonlight.

If only love
were the language of words

A thousand smiling suns in your stride
A thousand weeping stars in my pleas.

If only love
were the language of words

(From *Little Songs of Exile*, July 22, 1979)

I WISH I WERE WATER

To Maftoon Amini, poetry's kind fastidiousness

I wish I were water—
if one could be what one wants.

Being human
sigh!
is a trial at the limits of the impossible, don't you see?

I wish I were water, I tell myself—
to raise a slight sapling to a strapping tree
   (only to see it felled to earth
   by the wound of an axe to burn a fire?)
or to grant a feeble pine seedling everlasting greenness
   (before clump-staining it as a cross with
   pointless blood?)
or to be content from satiating the thirst of a parched pilgrim
   (even if he is made to kneel in the infernal
   field of sun and yowling to wait
   for the sword to his neck?
   Does it not baffle you:
   becoming Cain to your brother
   or executioner to Others
   or even to count a ripe-unripe tree
   as dead timber?).

I know, know, I know,
yet, I wish, oh I wish I were water,
if I could ever be what I wished for.

Ah
I wish I were still
     in all obliviousness
          a pure
drizzle drop of rain
          on the foothills
not a worthless wave
aimless in this tempestuous ocean of injustice.

(From *Unrewarded Eulogies*, September 21, 1989)

HAMLET

To be
or not to be…

That is not the question
that is the temptation.

—〰—

Poisoned wine in goblet and
venom-water-quenched sword

                    in the palm of the enemy's hand—

everything
is already clear and calculated
and the curtain

        will drop

             on cue.

Why, was it in the Garden of Gethsemane that my father fell asleep
that my lot is to inherit his betrayed trust,
and the bed of his betrayal,

             the seat of my uncle's pleasure!

(I realized all this

        at once

with a half-glance

        at the spectators

            at the start of the spectacle)

If only trust
            had not
like another demon
                    lulled to sleep this other, unaware Abel
in the other Gethsemane—
My god,
My god!

———〰———

But what deceit,
                    what deceit!
that the one watching from behind the half-faded
curtain of evil
is aware
of the entire tragedy
                    and already
knows
        word by word
my Gospel of Grief.

———〰———

The eyes
            behind the half-faded curtain of darkness
                        paid coins of silver and gold
to witness the spectacle of my anguish
to reap some pleasure
from the plot of open weeping
in the dissonance of voice and breath from the person
who pretends to doubt the truth.

What help would I want from these people who in the end
bow equally
          in respect
to my uncle and me before them,
even if my suffering was a clue to them that
Claudius
is no longer an uncle's name
but a universal notion.

And the curtain…
in the inevitable moment…

—⁓⁓—

Despite it all
          ever since the moment of truth
when a roaming, restless spirit revealed itself to me
and the world's stench
stung my nostrils
                    like the smoke of a flame in a farce
it has not been a question,
          but a temptation, this:

To be
or
not to be.

(From *Elegies of the Earth*, June 1969)

NELSON MANDELA

You are on the other side of the world in your burning cage
and I on this side,
and the line connecting us is untainted by time,
the shortest distance in the world.

Extend a hand in faith toward me
oh you neighbor in pain.

You are the glass globe over a trembling flame
against audacious wind
We are minstrels of forgotten praises, you and I
in tomes of scorn.
Presume not that you,
a high-seated guest in the tower of self-sacrifice,
are alone,
for all lovers
are kindred
not strangers.

Sing us a song in confidence
oh you neighbor in pain.

(From *Unrewarded Eulogies*, January 1989)

An Epic?

Nothing is happening at the intersection:
A few leave
A few return, exhausted.

And human—undoubtedly a god-like Fool[11] of old
—sells condoms
      joyless and hopeless
for two bites of bread
      at the crossroads of time.

A poet
      stood in the street
         and spontaneously wrote this epic
on the back of a pack of cigarettes:

"What I have to say is
Humans are gods.
Whether it is blasphemy or absolute truth, this word,
Humans are gods.
Yes, this is what I have to say!"

. . . .

The poet leapt, startled
from the horn of a lousy wretch of a bicyclist and…
         his pencil, its tip broke!

(From *Instants and Eternity*, December 19, 1960)

DARK SONG

The rider
is standing still
against the leaden backdrop of dawn
the long mane of his horse
        disheveled
in the wind.

—◊—

Oh Lord, oh Lord
riders are not to stand still
when the event
is imminent.

—◊—

The girl
is standing still
                by the burnt hedge
her thin skirt wavering

                        in the wind.

—◊—

Oh Lord, oh Lord
girls are not to stand still
when weary and hopeless
men
        grow old.

(From *Abraham in Flames,* 1973)

THE ANTHEM OF ABRAHAM IN FLAMES

For the execution of Mehdi Rezai at Chitgar Tir Square

In the bloodied ruin of light and dark
Behold a man transfigured[12]
who wanted the earth green
and love worthy of the fairest women
which to him
       seemed
not so worthless a gift
as to deserve gravel and stone.

What a man! What a man!
       who would say
the heart is more worthy

to bleed into earth

                        from the seven swords of love

and the throat better serving

the one who utters

               the most beautiful of names.

And a lion-iron-mountain of a man of such an ilk of lovers

trekked the blood-soaked battlefield of destiny

              on Achilles' heel—

an invincible-bodied

           whose secret of death

was the sorrow of love

and the grief of solitude.

                    —⟿—

"—Oh, sad Esfandiar![13]

better for you

that you avert your eyes!

                    —⟿—

"Was a *no*

        a single *no*

               enough

to forge my destiny?

I

alone cried,

            No!

I escaped

        the plunge.

I was a voice—
a form among forms—
and I gained a significance.

I was
and became,
not in the way that a bud

           a rose

or a root

           a sprout

or a single seed

           a forest—

but truly as
a common man

           a martyr

until the heavens pray before him.

—⁓—

I was not some helpless little submissive

           slave

And my celestial path to heaven
was not

      by a sheep-trail of fear and obedience:
I needed a different kind of god
worthy of a creature
whose neck

        would not crane

           for the inevitable scrap of bread.

And so
a different kind of god
I created."

—∿∿—

Alas, you lion-iron-mountain of a man

that you were,

and mountain-like you were
before falling to earth
steadfast and sturdy

already dead.

Yet, neither God, nor Satan

but an idol

wrote your destiny
that others

worshipped—
an idol that

others

worshipped.

(From *Abraham in Flames,* 1973)

RUPTURE

For the execution of Khosrow Golesorkhi

To be born
upon the dark spear
like the gaping birth of a wound.

To travel
                    the entire
tome of fortune
in chains.
To burn
          on one's own flame
down to the last spark,
on the light of veneration
such as found by slaves
in the dust
          of his way-worn path.

To blossom
this red and luring
          upon the thorn-bush of blood
and to cross
the thrashing-field of scorn
head held up so high
and to reach the ends of hatred.—

Ah, of whom do I speak?
We live unaware of why
They die well aware of why.

(From *Dagger in the Tray*, 1975)

FUNERAL ADDRESS

For Che Guevara

The unknowing are alike
Only the tempest breeds peerless children
Those alike are shadow-like
cautious on the fringes of sunlight
dead in the guise of the living.

And these
they are the throwers of caution to the wind
guardians of fires
the living shoulder to shoulder with death
marching ahead of death
forever alive after death
forever by the name with which they lived
for ruin passes under their towering vision
downcast and shamefaced
Discoverers of the fountainhead
humble discoverers of hemlock
seekers of joy in the volcanos' path
magicians of smiles in nightcaps of pain
with footprints deeper than joy
in flyways of birds
they brace thunder
enlighten the house
and die.

(From *Dagger in the Tray*, May 15, 1975)

IN THE MOMENT

I caress you and discover the world
I think of you and touch
time suspended
and boundless
naked.

I blow, I rain, I shine.
I am the sky
stars and the earth
and the fragrant wheat that
sprouts dancing
within its green self.

I pass through you as
thunder through night—

I glow
and implode.

(From *Little Songs of Exile*, 1980)

STILL LIFE

To Mitra Espahbod

A pile of paper
on the table
in the first glimpse of the sun.

An obscure book and
a burnt to ashes cigarette next to the forgotten cup of tea.

A forbidden matter
on the mind.

(From *At the Threshold*, December 1992)

GRAPPLING WITH SILENCE

1

I am *Daybreak,* in the end
weary
having waged war on no one but myself.

Albeit that no war is more grueling that this,
that even before galloping away on a horse
you are aware
that the enormous shadow of an open-winged vulture
has already crossed the field:
Fate has seared you blood-stained into the ground
and you can
no longer
escape
death and defeat.

I am *Daybreak*
A citizen of average height and wit
one generation away from wanderers of Kabul.
My first name is Arabic
my tribal name Turkic
my lineage Persian.
My tribal name is history's shame
and I dislike my first name
(only when you singsong it to me
this name is the world's most beautiful word
and that voice the saddest song of supplication).

I landed in this guesthouse of a world
on an unrelenting night of heavy snow
old and weary from the outset.

I was awaited in a bleak house
by the sacred mirrored fountain
near the mystic's temple.
(Perhaps why
I found the shadow of Satan
staking me out
from the outset).

At age five
I was still despondent from the unthinkable blow of my own birth
and grew up rootless
on salty sand
to the grunting of a drunk camel and the ghostly presence
of poisonous reptiles in a dust-bowl more remote
than the dusty memory of the last row of date palms
on the fringes of the last dry river.

At age five
I chased the image of a mirage in the naked dunes
empty gourd in hand
ahead of my sister
still a stranger to the magnetic pull of men.

I was six the first time I laid eyes
upon grief-stricken Abel receiving

a whipping from himself
public ceremony
in full befitting swing:
there was a row of soldiers, a pageant of cold,
silent chess pawns,
the glory of a dancing colorful flag
trumpets blasting and the life-consuming
rapping of drums
so Abel would not ail from the sound
of his own sobbing.

I am *Daybreak*
weary of warring with myself
weary of watering holes and temples and mirages
weary of deserts and whippings and commands
weary of Abel's shame of himself.
It is a long time now since I have uttered a word, but now
it is time to unleash, to bellow from the depths of my soul
for Satan has finally gripped me.

The row of cold infantry is bedecked
and the flag
of colorful majesty
flies at full staff.

The ceremonies are at peak perfection and completion
equal to the person they are for
to clip him like the smoking wick of a worthless candle
with shears.

They have stationed me across from the cold row
and the gold-stitched gag is ready
on a tin platter
beside a handful of basil and a fist-pounded onion.

When that bootlicking deputy emerges naked
the tempting beauty mark blasting the nation's brand
upon his shameful parts
and then the rap rapping of drums:
the ceremonies commence.

It is time for me to spit the whole of my hatred
in an endless yowl.
I am the first and the last *Daybreak*
I am Abel
upon the stage of degradation
I am the honor of the universe
whipped by myself
whose black fire of grief
out-shames hell for its measly riches.

2

In the hospital where my bed is an island
in the infinite vastness:
I scan every direction bewildered and perplexed:

This is not a tuberculosis ward.
The cancer patients and its female nurses fraternize
joylessly, by necessity.
Lepers with half-gnawed eyelids
and two hernial hearts ballooning in a bag
and a puddle of urine and flixweed in the veins
roam freely
with brooms of feather on spear-tips
dusting the devastation.

The hallways heavy with the feeling
of the shadow of a monster who commands silence
are the hub of dormitories with metal rings in stone walls
and whips and swords on the wall.
The diarrhea-afflicted
hang their shame in flowerbeds from a butcher's hook
and the heart of healing beats in the operating room
in a little tub of plasma waste and gauze
between the snoring of vultures under the operating table.

Here they prescribe leeches for healthy hearts
so you sing your heart out of the sweetest song of your life
to the brink of death

bright-eyed and bushy-tailed like a drunken canary
for you know
that safety
is a milky-kerneled corn
only rewarded in a cage,
so the lieutenant at the headquarters hands you safety papers
and a bottle of painkillers into the pocket of your gown:
one in the morning, one at night, with love!

———

Now the weary night passes the sanctuary of the mighty box trees
while in the kitchen
the surgeon's assistant
strips an unruly poet naked
to feed the head surgeon for breakfast
(anyone object?)

And the officially documented dead still have some fight
in them in the hearse headed to the graveyard
their pulses and tongues still
on fire pounding with fevered rage.

———

Naked, I am strapped down by the fours
on the operating table
but I must unleash a bellow
I am the honor of the universe after all
I am Abel
and the basin bowl of my skull
holds a morsel of a meal for the head surgeon.

With a bitter roar
I will turn the morsel into the serpent's venom in his mouth
I am *Daybreak,* after all
vanguard of the sun.

(From *Unrewarded Eulogies,* July 21, 1984)

NOCTURNE

No
I have not carved you from my longings:
more primeval than stone
more sprightly than a new blade of grass.

I have not drawn you out of my rage:
wisdom's inability

to emerge,

seething

at the furnace of restlessness.

I have not weighed you on the scales of my grief:
a blade of hay

in the pan of dispossession

a mountain

in measures of futility.

I have selected you
in spite of injustice
You said, *I love you*
and the rules

changed.

Do not settle, oh you command "of becoming"
Keep on becoming
Keep on becoming!

(From *Little Songs of Exile*, August 8, 1980)

EPITAPH

There was neither motion in leaving
Nor stillness in staying.

There was no severing of branches from roots
and the tale-telling wind
did not share any secrets with the leaves
as it should have.

The maiden of my love is an estranged mother
and the speeding star
orbits an eternal loop around
a hopeless track.

(From *Garden of Mirrors*, 1959)

BIRTH

Suddenly
sun-like
love
shed its mask

and filled the firmament
with the peal of appearance,
the lightning-like incandescence
subsided
and human
rose up.

(From *At the Threshold,* April 25, 1997)

AT THE THRESHOLD

One must stand tall and fall
at the threshold of a door without a knocker
for if your arrival is timely, the doorkeeper awaits you and

                                                          if untimely

there is no response to your pounding on the door.

The door is low
so better that you are humble
You could be a polished mirror

                                    there

to study
your graces

                     before entry
albeit that the commotion on the other side is a figment
of your own imagination and not in the actual crowd
for no one

                 awaits you

                       there.

For there may be

                 stirrings

                                  but nothing stirs to speak of:
no ghosts, or spirits, or saints with camphor in hand
no ghouls with fiery-headed bulls in fist
no maligned Satan with his party hat and its pompoms
no random amalgam of negating absolutes—
only you

               are an absolute being there,
pure being,

for you persevere in your own absence, and your absence
is the certain presence of miracles.
Your transit through the inevitable threshold
is the trickling of a drop of droplets in the infinite void:
"Alas,

     if only, if only

          there were

              judgment, judgment, judgment

                   to speak of!"

Perhaps if you had the powers of hearing
you would hear
the song of your trickling away in the silent hall of sunless galaxies
echo like the hurtling of ruin's regret:
"If only, if only

     a justice, justice, justice

          there, there, there, there…"

But a justice sits on the other side of the door
without the grim cloak of judges,
its nature compassion, fairness
its form time
and your memory shall be judged to eternal
eternity in the cycles of time to come.

―∿―

Farewell!
Farewell! (so says *Bamdad* the poet):
I dance through the threshold of duties
gladly and grateful.

I journeyed in from the outside:
from spectacle
to sport[14] to spectator—
not in the form of a sprout, not in the form of a butterfly,
not in the form of a rock, not in the form of a pool.
I was born in the form of "we"

                      in the glorious form of human
to sit gazing at the butterfly's rainbow in the sprout's spring
to discover the mountain's pride and hear the sea's splendor
to know my own purpose and to give
meaning to the world
by the measure of my own might and fortune
for a feat from these hands
is greater than the powers of birds, trees, cliffs, and waterfalls.

To be born human was the embodiment of duty:
the powers to love and be loved
the powers to hear
the powers to see and speak
the powers to feel sorrow and joy
the powers to laugh to the vastness of the heart
the powers to weep from the seat of the heart
the powers to lift a neck of pride in the majestic
heights of humility
the grand powers to shoulder the burden of trust
the somber powers to suffer loneliness
loneliness
loneliness
naked loneliness.

To be human
is the difficulty of the duty.

—∿—

My bound hands were not free for me to embrace every scene
every song, every spring and sparrow
every full moon and every first light of dawn
every peak and tree and other human.
I crossed the chance to live with cuffed hands shut mouth
we crossed hands and mouth shut
and we only saw
the spectacle that is this world
through the mean-spirited crack in the prison wall of wickedness
                                        and now
that low, knocker-less door before us and
that gesture of the awaiting doorkeeper!—

I have journeyed through a tight passageway
I gaze back at parting
                to fare well:

Time was brief and the journey grueling
But it was singular and lacked nothing.

I swear with all my indebted and grateful being!
(so said *Bamdad* the weary).

(From *At the Threshold*, November 20, 1992)

I Cannot Not Be Beautiful

I cannot not be beautiful
not be a flirtation in infinite revelation.

I am so beautiful
that spring unconsciously graces my passage:

In my world
blood is never
the spirit disrobed
and the dread of lead
does not dissuade the partridge
from its stride.

I am so beautiful
that *Allah o Akbar* or *God is Great*
is inevitably your description
of me.
I am poison without antidote before you.
If the world is beautiful
it is waxing poetic about me—

You imbecile,[15] you
I am not your rival
I am your very denial!

(From *Unrewarded Eulogies*, 1983)

16. VENOM OF SNAKE

O NE AFTERNOON IN OCTOBER 2014, I checked my email as I was entering a walk-up apartment building during a visit to New York City and found a curious email from the publisher of a journal to me and CC'd to a colleague I knew, but it addressed me in the third person to the colleague. I scrolled down to the bottom to find an email chain, a conversation about my work that was being conducted without me.

The colleague had initiated an email to the publisher to say that following a citation of the Official Website of Ahmad Shamlou, which they maintained, had taken them to the journal's website, and they were wondering whether "the translator" had shown evidence of permission to publish her translation online, because colleague was the sole copyright holder of all of the Shamlou works published electronically, and they had not granted me permission.

I had befriended this colleague on Facebook in December 2013, being that we had literary friends in common and whose name I had noticed in remote relation to Shamlou. Curious to learn more about colleague's work, I proposed that we chat by phone. When we did, they were complimentary of my work, even sent me a link (which has since disappeared) to their positive review of my translations in my anthology, *Belonging*. They also emailed me a link to the Shamlou timeline arranged by Mrs. Shamlou and a few other tidbits. They told me they maintained the Official Website of Ahmad Shamlou. I told them about my plan to incrementally work on a Shamlou project and asked if they could be a resource if I needed one. They happily offered any help they could provide.

A couple of months later, colleague told me that they were traveling to the U.S. in March 2014 to attend the Association of Writers and Writing Programs (AWP) conference in Seattle. Our first in-person meeting happened just before colleague's panel. I was heartened by their warmth and friendliness. After the panel we made plans to meet the next day. Colleague was coming to the conference center from off-site accommodations and was late. They bragged of having spent the previous night inebriated on a whole bottle of something hard, but we began chatting about Shamlou. We were joined mid-conversation by others dropping by. Then we browsed the book fair with our group and at some point we were talking together again. They said they have access to some of Shamlou's unpublished letters and other materials they could put at my disposal should I want them, repeatedly offering any help I might need in my project. *I'll help you any way I can, anytime.* Then they were abruptly whisked away, mid-sentence it seemed, by a Collaborator of colleague's who saw us talking from afar, and I did not see colleague again.

It was disorienting to receive this email chain, only seven months after such offers of help. In the interim, I had won a fellowship for my translations of Shamlou's works, it had been announced, and the publisher of the aforementioned literary journal, where the only translation of Shamlou's work I had published after going through a rigorous round of edits, suggested they link to the print work as a way to celebrate my award. I agreed. I wrote a brief bio of Shamlou for the journal's webpage and linked it to the Official Website of Ahmad Shamlou. Despite the fact that the site is in Persian, I thought more traffic to that site by both readers of Persian and English would be beneficial in raising awareness of the enormity of Shamlou's legacy.

My tongue swelled as I was processing the email and trying to make sense of WHAT HAD JUST HAPPENED. My mouth contracted into a ring of wrinkles, a sea urchin, my heart leaping ferociously, my breathing audible and shallow, my vision went abstract, sweat formed on my brow, my upper lip, and my body broke out in a silent siren. I recalled colleague's earnest eyes and collegial offers. So why email the publisher without writing me first?

Adrenaline pumping, I composed my response email on the ascent to the sixth floor, and before sliding the key into the lock, I had sent it off.

We went back and forth within a matter of minutes, colleague still addressing the publisher while really communicating with me. Colleague pasted into an email a paragraph that they claimed was (the translation of) part of the contract with Shamlou that gave them exclusive rights to the poet's work in electronic form when they began maintaining the poet's website, a new and exciting electronic platform in the 1990s.

Googling Ahmad Shamlou's name, in just one spelling (Shamlou), and not in alternate spellings, such as Shamlu, Shamloo, or in the Persian and other languages, yields millions of hits. I wondered whether all the people posting online had asked for and received permission from colleague to post poems, tributes, translations, photos, audio clips, and videos of Shamlou. More importantly, had colleague policed them all?

In the email exchange, I wrote that the rights granted to me by Mrs. Shamlou were all-inclusive, that in fact I had to have these rights for my fellowship award application.

For my award application, I wrote.
Really, REALLY SMART move.
Because, basically, I was disoriented.

Have you ever felt your fight or flight instinct?

I have. Once when I was mugged while kissing my date goodbye leaning against my car at 2 a.m.

A car had driven by and grabbed my silly little red purse that dangled off my arm as my head was in the clouds, and had sped off. And I had gone with the purse, catapulted into the air and dragged skin to asphalt. When I finally let go of the strap, I got up a different creature, like The Terminator, and marched toward my car without skipping a beat or feeling anything. I heard a remote voice totally unknown to me rise from some deep pipe in my body, *GET IN THE CAR!*

YES, MA'AM, said my petrified Midwestern farm boy transplant of a date with the roundest eyes ever. Welcome to city life, baby! I pedaled to the metal through EVERY red light on Mission Street in pursuit and when I saw patrol cars at 16th Street, a.k.a. crack central, the guttural voice commanding from a different dimension blurted from the window of my speeding car that did not slow down, *FOLLOW ME!* which the officers instantly scurried to do. I escorted the police through many red lights until I decided I lost the getaway car—or maybe the car was never in sight to begin with—and pulled over. When the alarmed cops hurried to my window, they repeatedly asked whether they could take me to the hospital. I kept asking why.

Only after we got back to my apartment, somehow, two hours that I cannot account for later, did I notice that my knee was mauled, bleeding everywhere. I was too shocked to make it to the ER. So was farm boy, who was uninjured but likely deciding to move back to Ohio or Iowa right then and there. I have a little war wound next to other scab marks from when I was a little girl to remind me of the savage Incredible Hulk beast that lives inside me.

That might begin to describe the flood of adrenaline that October day on the sixth floor in NYC.

Inside the apartment, disregarding the time difference in Karaj, I called Mrs. Shamlou and explained what had happened, asking whether all electronic publishing rights did in fact belong to this colleague. She lost her temper: *"We haven't seen [colleague] in twelve years! They have no rights. That contract is outdated and is being nullified. Your translation was well done, placed in a respectable journal befitting the poet! This is a clear act of sabotage!"*

I wrote a separate email to colleague asking to discuss this new development, but did not hear back.

Not twenty-four hours later, Mrs. Shamlou wrote me an email stating that I had betrayed her trust, misrepresented our agreement. That she had told me electronic rights were to be granted by the Official Website. I did not recall that, or I would have discussed this with colleague upon meeting them. Nor had there been any information on the Official Website about the procedures to obtaining permission for electronic publications.

Mrs. Shamlou stated that the rights she had signed off on for my award application were for traditional print publishing, and not for electronic forms, and not all-inclusive.

When I had first contacted Mrs. Shamlou, I had asked for rights to Shamlou's entire body of work in order to have free rein as I studied and whittled down what I wanted to include in my "Shamlou Reader." She informed me that the members of the institute that runs the Shamlou estate, the Alef. Bamdad Institute, had deliberated and were not comfortable at that time to grant rights to the *entire* body of work, but that I could submit a list of specific works, which I did and informed her that I was submitting my translations for a fellowship. I followed their own directions, and Mrs. Shamlou sent me a signed letter granting me the right to translate and publish the fifty works I had listed. My plan was to later expand the scope of permissions to include performance and other rights, but at that time, I wanted just to meet the award deadline, which required translation and publication rights.

Mrs. Shamlou then went on to write that there were errors in my translation of *"Collective Love,"* that I had failed to identify the article in the first stanza as indefinite.

Mrs. Shamlou does not speak English. The nouns in the first two lines were in fact pluralized and left without any articles in order to read better in the English ("Tears are a mystery/Smiles a mystery" versus "The tear is a mystery/The smile is a mystery"). This must have been reported to her by colleague as a cardinal sin and proof of my ineptitude as a translator. But a person in her position, having lived with a prolific and opinionated translator, would be familiar with the myriad considerations that go into the decisions of translating a line within a larger poem. So I wondered: Why the sudden criticism?

She had pasted two Shamlou quotes about translation, one from Shamlou's article questioning whether the translator's social commitment suffices for literary work, and the other against word-by-word translation of poetry, which I thought only proved that my approach was spot-on. She said that the task of translating poetry is a grave responsibility, and the translated poem must be inspected by one or two poets in the target language to verify its poeticity. This sounded like the mantle of "only poets could and should translate poets," a familiar slogan I had encountered amongst a small number of translators from the Persian. Their platform had always begged two questions: 1) Are mediocre poets qualified to translate great poets? 2) Does it matter who translates a poem as long as the resultant translation is a poem? Because I have read a number of translations of *"Collective Love,"* for example, by "poets" whose translations could, at best, be read as awkward and incorrect English.

In my own translation practice, the intent is to reconstruct the original poem from scratch, from complete erasure, working to meet the innovations, images, style, and musicality of the original, building a new poem that reaches as close to 100 percent of the original—in its own way. Shamlou knew this would never be achieved with a straightforward approach, but rather with careful and artful tending to. It is craft (math) plus alchemy (art).

This approach to translation is commonly held by professional translators worldwide and not exclusive to Shamlou, or to me. Most translators fall somewhere on the spectrum of fidelity to the spirit and innovation of the original text and a less successful literal rendition of it.

I wondered how Mrs. Shamlou had acquired a sudden expert opinion on my English translation, which had gone through a rigorous editorial process before publication in the literary journal, not to mention passed the two-step review process of the award in question, first read by an original-language reader for fidelity, then by a target-language reader for ingenuity in English—why the award is an important and serious one.

Then again, the Incredible Hulk savage in me had written that I had "all-inclusive rights" when my human head was exploding with the urge to call colleague—who wrote such an undermining email—to say, *What's up, friend?!*

I contacted editors and publishers and translators who had translated and published works by Shamlou in the U.S., both in print and online, asking whether they had secured any rights and how. No response from one, evasion from another. Only one editor discussed it, citing the fact of a nonexistent copyright relationship between Iran and the United States for giving free rein to translate and publish in any form. The same editor also warned me that colleague could jeopardize my fellowship award.

I thought, one of the self-proclaimed upholders of Shamlou's legacy and a website ruining exposure of the poet's work in award-winning translation? It was such a farfetched idea to me that I gallantly went, *Pffft, the award?! NAH.*

To ruin something for someone.

So much has been ruined for me:

- An Andras Schiff Bach Suites concert I had looked forward to ruined by the large man next to me breathing so loudly that I had to run, fist to chest, up the aisle mid-concert to exit the hall. (Probably not intentional.)

- Wonton soup containing a long strand of thick grey hair. (Not intentional.)

- My invitation by an Iranian student body at Stanford University because the professor funding their activities refused to support it. (Probably intentional.)

- The revocation of my fifth translation award, this one for translating Shamlou's poetry, a few weeks later. (Definitely intentional.)

I suppose "revocation" is not precise wording. My translations did pass the panel's rigorous two-step review, and winners were publicly announced, but I never received the award money. So maybe this was a rescindment? Either way, $12,500 vanished.

I was told by the distraught award director—who had also personally called me only four months earlier to congratulate me on my win—that, to her knowledge, this had never happened in the history of the award.

So I was the first.

Not only the first to win a translation award at all for translating this poet, I think, but also for being the only winner in the award's history for translating contemporary Iranian literature—the only (two) previous wins were for Medieval Persian poetry.

The award staff had reportedly jumped up and down in excitement when the panel decided to award my work because not only did they love the poems, but they had also been privy to the lengths I had gone to in order to obtain a signed letter from Mrs. Shamlou granting me translation and publishing rights.

Mrs. Shamlou had suddenly stopped answering her telephone around the award application deadline and the staff had generously given me an extension until it was absolute time for the panel to review the completed applications.

Fortunately, I was able to reach Mrs. Shamlou in time, in January 2014, and obtained written permission for fifty poems (nine of which I submitted for the award), and my application was deemed complete. Upon winning, I was invited to be featured on the award's website with a bio and sample translation of Shamlou's work. A translator gets support to complete a book of translations, and a world-class poet receives an introduction and readership in a new language. A win-win for everyone.

But apparently not.

Happy Eurydice, after marrying her Orpheus, was chased and bitten by a snake and sent to the underworld.

Jesus, too, was bitten. By Judas, a snake in his own right. The story of Jesus' anguish in the garden of Gethsemane, before his arrest and crucifixion following Judas' betrayal, is considered to be one of the more provocative passages in the Gospels. This is the moment that launches the Passion of Christ. Following his sermon at the Last Supper, Jesus and three disciples enter the garden at the foot of the Mount of Olives in Jerusalem. Jesus prays at the mount. He has a premonition about his fate and experiences a spectrum of feelings: agony, doubt, sorrow, terror, turmoil. An angel descends from the heavens to comfort him. Coming to terms with his fate, he is torn as a human, "the spirit is willing, but the flesh is weak" (Mark 14:38). His agony as he prayed was such that "his sweat became like great drops of blood falling down upon the ground" (Luke 22:44).

This exercise of will and commitment is the subject of a body of paintings, generally named *Agony in the Garden*. In these paintings, the tableau also depicts Judas and the angry mob of Jews approaching in the distance to apprehend Jesus and turn him in to Pontius Pilate, the final chapter of Jesus' public trial and willingness to suffer and die on the cross.

Silence is an animal with two faces:

2.   To be silenced by someone else is to be robbed. It is the death of the self, a corpse lodged in the embankment of a river, tossing against the jagged edge, bloated, splayed open to be gawked at by the proud living unaware that the other side is a mere email away.

The agony of existing in the body is matched by the euphoria in its abandon to pleasures. I am too present in my body, bound to its demands, its minute yearnings—now you are hot, now you are ever-so-slightly nauseous, now your shooting neck pain strikes, now your bladder, now you blow your nose, now you sit, but the corner of the chair pokes into the back of your thigh, now clip your shoulders like an angel to sit up, now scratch your elbow, now four thoughts and chores cross your mind, now run to pull out that bill from your wallet, now you remember an inane conversation, an animosity, now your demons grandstand, now you perk up and breathe, now you are bumped a galaxy away from where you ought to be, now you are despondent because three minutes have passed, now three hours, and you have done a round-robin of this routine, unable to gather your mind, and now you decide enough is enough, it is time to change scenery.

17. TO COLLEAGUE, MY CENSOR

YOU USED TO BE ON MY MIND ALL THE TIME. More than that, you were also in my blood. In my dreams. And when I suddenly remembered *it*, what you did to me, that horrid phone call about my award, all those months mute and lost and striving for an answer. You were also on my mind when I was trying to be good and chew the broccoli stalk and not just the spongy florets, because we really pay for that heavy stalk. My throat would constrict and then my eyes and sinuses would flood with *saltsting*.

It was the *mostalonest* I ever felt in the world. My pen also froze.

You shattered my sense of self. I was in a state of insomnia and a simultaneous recurring nightmare that I could not wake from. My heart kept sinking into my bowels. A sense of powerlessness gripped me, more disorienting than when I lost control of my car on the 405 freeway, unable to pilot the steering wheel. Language can no more cover the devastation I felt than weeping expressed the depth of my desolation. I wondered, *how did I get here, to be a person upon whom this venom is spewed?* I drifted explanation-less around some orbit of hell since the call from the awarding institution that came just as I had sat in my car on a warm day to drive away, but instead sat still under a cascade of pin-pricks coursing down my body. My throat retched as I whimpered to another adult—the distressed caller who said this had never happened in the history of the institution—stuttering in protest, a sniveling stranger to myself.

For a long time, I found it impossible to tell this story. You silenced me on many levels. I could not visit with friends, nor could I adequately explain why. My systems shut down. Rebecca Solnit wrote in *The Mother of All Questions* that silencing strips a person of their humanity. Those who are heard move to the center. Others are cast out. Silence separates rather than unites. Being unable to tell your story is a living death.

Eight months of my life vanished reaching out to you and complete strangers worldwide trying to make sense of your intentions, researching the complex maze of international copyright law, seeking pro-bono legal help, composing long emails to the awarding institution, calling and writing the estate, weeping in many therapy sessions, pacing my apartment in the middle of the night, finding myself in a crusted dribble of snot on the bare floor in the morning, scrambling to pull myself back up from the shores of shame.

My shame. Overwhelming as Magritte's corpulent and silent green apple taking up an entire room in his 1952 painting, *Listening Room*.

I think I can say that you divided my life into two: Before Censor. After Censor. I divide it up differently now.

You helped me. I'm not going to be brazen and say I did not pay for my superpowers. Oh, no, I paid dearly. I had to die first, then be in a state of numbness. I had to feel like a million maggots had laid eggs in my mouth, a much uglier condition than the moth smothering the victims' voice boxes in *Silence of the Lambs*. That scenario seems pristine, almost romantic. The maggots reproduced in my mouth for a long time. I was nauseous. Ashamed. What if someone saw what my mouth had come to? I dared not open it lest they brand me maggot-mouth. Stranger angels popped up to prop me up. My *strangels*. They saw deep into ugly, broken me. They buoyed me, life rafts when my boat had capsized. All the while, though, I felt like a whiner on the victim-me sermon trail. Like now. A punishment in itself.

I kept replaying my history with you, looking for the Trojan horse I had missed. I doubted and second-guessed myself. I thought I was raving mad. Was I being gaslighted? The shame grew and so did my distance from the world until it was just me and my handful of polite listeners and my hallucinations. And grief: the loss of my poet, my project, my dignity, my mastery of my little world. You go into full-blown mourning for something you cannot divulge at large, and hence, more alienation. Then, paranoia and suspicion. You think everyone somehow knows you are disgusting and unlovable and is going to abandon you if they have not already in order to be on the other side. On your side. Because you were holstered up, shiny brass on the rise, the almighty expert. The ball was in your court since you seized the entire field.

You probably already know all of this, but the Alef. Bamdad Institute put me through an inquisition. I went down a rabbit hole, trying to reason with several people there who treated me with suspicion, not only because of the recent misunderstanding, but also, it seemed to me, because I was based in the United States, by virtue of which they likely found me flush with cash and deceit. Gave new meaning to LOST IN TRANSLATION. We had circular conversations and I came to understand that they had never received the draft of my translations Mrs. Shamlou had asked for when signing my permission letter in January 2014, which I had immediately sent. No forwarding of my Sent Email confirmations from my actual Gmail account convinced them, and they began to claim that they would have never allowed me to submit translations to a fellowship without their approval. They said they wanted to conduct an "independent review" of my work.

I thought, by this logic, if the translations were approved, I might have a chance still to recover my award with one follow-up email from them confirming that they have, in fact, approved my work and granted me permission, even if this order of things would seem bizarre to the awarding institution (though this would not be the first time Iranians embarrass Iranians). In re-forwarding my translations to the estate, I noted that their English language fluency would likely be in a different version of the actual written and spoken English in the United States, which could compromise their assessment. They believed their English to be "good enough." Some weeks later, I asked for and received confirmation that a third-party reviewer had deemed my translations accurate and approved.

A glimmer of hope, I thought. One email from the estate would clear up the whole mess.

But no one took action. I decided to reach the co-inheritor with Mrs. Shamlou of the Shamlou estate, Mr. X. The contact numbers given to me by Mrs. Shamlou's office were dead ends. After calling complete strangers I thought were associated with Mr. X, whose numbers I found on the internet, I was able to reach Mr. X. Mrs. Shamlou and he were known to maintain a public alliance of necessity and convenience against all other fronts, but theirs was a game of chess, of tense power dynamics.

When I finally reached Mr. X and introduced myself, I had to strain to hear him, a voice not rising to reach me. Fair enough, here is an old man being contacted out of the blue by who I thought could be a stranger to him then. Little did I know, and I would find out later, that he was CC'd on the email you wrote to the awarding institution, the only person from the estate to be CC'd. Not Mrs. Shamlou, who was my point of contact at the estate, and who had signed and sent my letter granting rights, and therefore the logical person to be in the loop.

Mr. X began to lecture me unprompted about translation. He said he had not looked over my work, nor was he interested in the third-party reviewer's verdict on my translations. I wondered why the estate had asked for it then. He said that in order to get his personal permission for translating Shamlou, I would have to gain his trust by writing "hundreds of times," maybe "25-page-long emails analyzing each line of poetry," until he was satisfied. Then I would have to send my English renditions. He said that though he spoke English, his English was not appropriate for assessments, nor would he want to meddle in my renditions, yet he would want to approve my translations. So which was it? It is reasonable up to a certain point for estates to monitor, but he had pushed everything into such confusion that it was a parody of itself.

At some point in this process, I began to realize that you and Mr. X are from the same village. In fact, someone close to the estate mentioned that Mr. X is your uncle.

In the spring of 2015, you responded to another request of mine to talk. But you did not answer Skype each time I tried. After several attempts, I was able to reach you. I opened with a smile and said I wanted to have an amiable conversation about the issue. Imagine my state. You nodded. I first had to sit through you rambling on and on about your own life and accomplishments when all I wanted to do was get to the point, but, no, I had opened by saying I wanted to be pleasant, and since I wanted to do nothing to seem, I don't know, on the defensive, or betrayed and broken, I nodded and smiled. It reminded me of how I treated the person who had assaulted me in college. Nice and pleasant.

You said your policing efforts extend only to professional translators, not to amateurs, whom you called "propagandists." Only "inferior" translations are to get air and ether time, then? I fail to see the logic. I have yet to hear about other professional translators being subjected to this policing. Or maybe we are all hiding in shame. You derided Americans for not having international vision, particularly when it comes to literature. I thought, that, and leveraging the awarding institution's lack of fluency in Persian and access to Iran, and whatever was holding back Mrs. Shamlou, was a perfect storm for you to make a move, manipulate, grandstand. Then you boasted of having publishers at the ready in several countries to publish your work. I found it odd to pour salt over the wound of someone you have just stripped of an award, publishing credit and opportunities, and online features.

Letters were sent to the awarding institution by U.S.- and Europe-based publishers, and leadership in the American Literary Translators Association, to which I have belonged since 2005 and from which I received a translation fellowship years ago. But the awarding institution sent a form letter that stated this was a closed matter and would not be discussed with third parties. It was never discussed with me either. The only correspondence I received from the office of general counsel was in June 2015 explaining their position and attaching a copy of your email to them (a long, charming read!) after I had invoked the Freedom of Information Act. This is when I saw who had, and who had not, been CC'd on your fateful letter.

Over time, weighing what was being asked of me, and the bitter taste the experience had left, I decided not to work under the conditions of and treatment by Mr. X and the Alef. Bamdad Institute. I imagine few translators would. I could, and did, find others with whom to read and analyze the poetry without expectations that I adhere to their interpretations, and most importantly, English renditions. It seemed you all were inventing nonexistent protocol, winging it as you went along to achieve your end, whatever that was. A stonewalling.

We humans and our autoimmune diseases. We Cains and Abels.

I imagine that the Shamlou estate tries in earnest to establish and follow protocol, be organized. But in a country that persecutes its own sons and daughters, the spirit of censorship and self-mutilation echoes in relationships. Could it be that the devastating effect of constant surveillance, persecution, censorship, and self-censorship has petrified Iranians into a perpetual combative state? God knows, you have your own open letters from various quarters questioning your claims and publishing activities of Shamlou's work to contend with.

Your actions disrupted the narrative and flow of my life and self. I wanted to appear brimming with confidence and certainty about what really happened. I never felt heroic or brazen or even elevated to the status of "censored writer," which has its own cachet, like your "poet in exile." I tried many times to tell my story. I would lose momentum toward the end, wondering who cared about the details, and yet yearning to leave a document. I doubted my own story, finding myself suddenly on the defensive, an unreliable character, pressured to prove my intentions. Being that I conditioned female, I spent years questioning myself, wondering what I must have done wrong, I mean, aside from writing that email while hauling up six flights of stairs when a black vortex swirled before my eyes. But in hindsight, I see that questioning my rash email was senseless because YOU HAD ALREADY UNDERMINED me by emailing the literary journal questioning the actions of "the translator." My name is Niloufar, and you knew me. And you had offered support.

You had already undermined me by public-shaming me in the view of the awarding institution, all the people I confided in, all the people who wrote letters pleading with you to consider the ramification of your actions. I was already soiled by the stain of your accusation, by the ugliness with which you denounced me, calling me "deceitful and cunning" in your letters, Hester Prynne branded with a scarlet C, Censored, Cunning.

You had already undermined me when I had to go from conference to conference with the cloak of shame on me, whispering my sob story to leaders in the translation world, some of whom rolled their eyes in horror that I had dared to air dirty cultural laundry when I tried to speak about the erasure of cultures from within, at the hands of arbiters with an agenda, when I dared to wonder how one of the nation's higher institutions would rescind an award without vetting the accuser of an applicant they had worked with for months, one they wanted to feature, they rolled their eyes and distanced themselves from the *castaside* because these things upset public decorum. You had already undermined me when the dishonor in such treatments, foreign to so many, left my husband in confusion, irritation, and eventually angry at me.

You had already undermined me when I could no longer spend time with people because there was this tumor in my throat that I could not speak of, and yet I could not speak of anything else, so I was a dead wooden figure to them. My awareness was laced with a bitter tonic, my outlook acidic. You had already undermined me when I was spending time in the ER under a battery of tests for not being able to breathe (test results: inconclusive—*but I can't breathe*) instead of translating our literature, our Shamlou. You had already undermined me when I retroactively called into question everything I had ever done, my very own integrity, when you stripped from me the tiny shred of validation and visibility I received from "the establishment." You had already divested me and EVERY SINGLE TRANSLATOR who would come after me, my future colleagues, of a place at the little table of translation to translate ANYONE from the Persian because we are CAINS killing ourselves and why should anyone else care, because we are not WINNERS, not even you. Award after award, I see no books translated from the Persian on any list.

WHY DO YOU THINK THAT IS?

We will have NO LEGACY, and that is YOUR legacy.

You had already undermined me by writing to the awarding institution that the Alef. Bamdad Institute supervises contracts for Shamlou's heirs, including Mrs. Shamlou, and it had not granted me permission, implying that Mrs. Shamlou's permission to me was not official or executed through the institute. Mrs. Shamlou told me in that October 2014 phone call that at the time she granted me permission with her January 2014 emailed letter, she herself had the authority to do so. In any case, because the decision to grant me permission for fifty works versus Shamlou's entire body of work was made collectively, I imagined the institute was always in the loop.

You later made sloppy claims to others who wrote you to reconsider your actions:

"From our readings of few of [Did you mean 'a few of'?] her translations published online, it was our concern that she was unable to understand the poems and had not sought help to do so either."

I had only published one (*"Collective Love"*), not several, as you claim, and the awarding institution's first-round native reader approved them, not to mention the Alef. Bamdad Institute's own third-party reader later. You churn out one, sometimes more translations a day. You, a "poet," did not even bother to turn your rendition of *"Collective Love"* into a poem in accurate English—it looked as if you spent fifteen minutes on it. How do you work such fast magic?

You also wrote: "Despite Mr. [I'm a Ms., but I like your attention to detail] Talebi's underhanded methods to gain sympathy and cast our institute in a negative light (which I must say, is very disturbing to us all), we are still open to any capable translator who wishes to work with our organization in a positive and honest manner. If she proves herself capable, we are willing to work with her. She is and has been for a long time fully aware of that. Why she has chosen not to share the true status of the situation with you is beyond me."

Colleague, my censor, what happened between the last time I saw you at AWP in March 2014 and when you began your campaign of shame in October 2014? How could I ever know the truth of things, my information fragmentary, scant, my take of things skewed, and the truth so subjective?

We communicate by signs. Somerset Maugham wrote in his *Moon and Sixpence:* "…and the signs have no common value, so that their sense is vague and uncertain. We seek pitifully to convey to others the treasures of our heart, but they have not the power to accept them, and so we go lonely, side by side but not together, unable to know our fellows and unknown by them…I do not know what infinite yearning possesses you, so that you are driven to a perilous, lonely search for some goal where you expect to find a final release from the spirit that torments you. I see you as the eternal pilgrim to some shrine that perhaps does not exist. I do not know to what inscrutable Nirvana you aim. Do you know yourself? Perhaps it is Truth and Freedom that you seek, and for a moment you thought that you might find release in Love."

Edith Grossman, the acclaimed translator of Gabriel García Márquez, Mario Vargas Llosa, Carlos Fuentes, and many others, whose translation of *Don Quixote* is widely considered to be a masterpiece, quotes Lorraine Adams from her January 6, 2008, *Book Review of the New York Times* piece in her book, *Why Translation Matters*: "Literature in translation, regardless of its origin, has trouble finding American publishers. The languages of Islam, unlike European languages, particularly French and Spanish, are not often spoken or read by American editors. 'When you have a book proposal, you have to have at least two chapters and a synopsis in English,' explained Nahid Mozaffari, an Iranian historian who edited *Strange Times, My Dear,* a 2005 PEN anthology of contemporary Iranian literature. 'But there is no money to pay for translation. A lot of what's happening is [that] nostalgic exiles or academics…[are] doing the chapter and synopsis in their spare time. Not all of them are good writers, and [a lot] of literature has been killed by bad translation…'" Yet you decided to block an experienced translator.

Each time I dug deep to construct my story as a coherent narrative, I could not find the language. I was in a fugue from despair to hope and back, a Sisyphean cycle. It remained a silent scream. I fought to invent new language to convey the violence. Then I remembered Cain and Abel. So it was just new to me.

And then I realized that being silenced was not new to me. Your hellfire-lightning just broke a dam. The tsunami hurling me made me *see* the translucent lake of silence I had been in all along, being shushed, talked over, ignored, diminished. I had mistaken those reflections in that glass-like surface as myself. Once I saw the lake, I gasped into rebellion. I was born.

I used to wake in the morning after an interrupted night of sleep or no sleep to troubling thoughts or my mind racing with some alarm. A far cry from being woken up on lazy weekend mornings in my teenage bed from the sound of my father gently rapping his fingers on my bedroom door, whistling a nightingale's song.

Almost twenty years after the censorship by Raymond Queneau and Jacques Lemarchand, members of the publisher Gallimard's reading committee, of the most sincere parts of the French writer Violette Leduc's book, *Ravages*, for fear that it would become a scandal, Leduc movingly pleaded her cause in *La Chasse à L'amour* (*The Hunt for Love*), a posthumous part of her autobiographical trilogy: "Where is censure's true home? What are her habits, her manias? I can't work her out. I was building a school...a dormitory...a refectory...a music room...a courtyard...Each brick, an emotion. Each rafter, an upheaval. My trowel digging up memories. My mortar to seal in the sensations. My building was solid. My building is collapsing. Censure has pushed my house over with the tip of one finger. I had a pain in my chest the day I learned of their rejection. I was wounded right in my heart. Society opposes it even before my book can be published. My work is broken up, scattered. My searching through the darkness of memory for the magical eye of a breast, for the face, the flower, the meat of a woman's open sex...My searching, a box of empty bandages. Continue to write after such a rejection? I cannot. Stumps keep poking out of my skin."[16]

Me too, colleague, idea by idea, stone by stone, I was building my cathedral, its doors, windows, vaulted ceilings. My cathedral collapsed too. You, my censor, failed to realize that by demolishing my structure, you also weakened your own. You are not you, you are no one, your name is Censure.

Silence is the universal condition of oppression. It is a crime of control, exclusion, humiliation, devaluation, deprivation of agency. In silencing me, you self-mutilated, self-silenced, even if your own voice moves to the center—for some time. When young translators write me asking questions about rights, sources of support, leads in the publishing world, whether I could collaborate, connect them to Mrs. Shamlou, what is there to tell them? How many translators into just English do Rilke and Neruda have? Those translations speak to and interact with each other.

Their readers can exercise choice, enjoy comparative readings. In other words, more is more in translation. Even the presence of less professional and successful translations is better if it ignites the desire in someone to better translate an author.

Christopher Hitchens wrote of "assassins of the mind" in his essay about the collateral damage of Ayatollah Khomeini's fatwa on Salman Rushdie for writing *Satanic Verses*. When accused, silencers fight back with harsh words and accusations, deflecting the real issue of real brutality. The silenced opt for privacy. Bullies rely upon that.

The damage by so-called Advocates of Persian Literature who claim unvetted ownership of authors, effectively creating a state of siege for our literature, is grave. Without context as to the marginality of Iranian literature in translation, this was an act of literary thuggery. But with context, it's cataclysmic.

Beyond the personal pain that it cost and continues to cost me, my silence would perpetuate a collective erasure, consent to a continual colonization of my native tongue and literature, maintain the Policed State of Mind. It would keep translators from the Persian powerless. It would be against ambassadorship.

My last few exchanges with Mrs. Shamlou do not dismay me. She was tempered, eloquent, maintained boundaries decades ago when I called her Auntie Aida in my family's home and later, when her actions, or rather, silence, baffled me. No doubt reactive and spent from waging war for four decades alongside Shamlou, and ongoing on his behalf for two decades since his death, it is a marvel that she has any fight left in her. The only time I ever heard her lose her temper was when I called her after receiving your October 2014 emails.

That Shamlou is not widely read in the West has much to do with the fact that his work, though it was in conversation with international art, was deeply rooted in its cultural context and language, which renders his work a challenge to bridge over, but not impossible. The great artists belong to the world. May readers find all our books, existing translations, mine, and even your possible future book, my censor. May they read and enjoy them all, generously, comparatively. May they be born anew generation after generation as budding translators—for translators are born of love.

18. TIME, A LONG, LONG, TIME (THROUGH THE FIRE)

LIKE **PAVLOV'S DOG,** each time I heard of or thought of Shamlou, I felt stabbed. Red for wound.

In what Joan Didion called "an act of disrespect for the self," I grew a Talented Mr. Self-Pity. I spent ruined days and nights tallying my defeats, the ways I had been wronged, or at least thought I had been, measuring the scorn directed at me.

But I also imagined for fleeting moments what could be possible when there is a little, if not a lot of, love and push and padding and platform and voice, away from the tinge of scandal, the stink of *castaside*. I could almost feel how I would float like figures in a Chagall painting, how different every thing, every moment would be.

I trusted that given time, one day I would reassemble my self. *This too shall pass,* I thought. So I waited. And time passed, washed away the sting of the poisoned arrow, mended the exit wound of treachery. The unfathomable pain subsided. I emerged from that tunnel.

In all my powerlessness, my immeasurable advantage was knowing that my pain came from the story I told myself about these sets of events. I chose to reassess and reassign their value, overwrite my silence to create my own limitless life.

I once saw a cartoon showing a prison guard surrounded by darkness looking through the peephole into a cell to see a prisoner sitting at the edge of a vast open sea with a thought bubble. Who was the free person? I must first get past the prison of my own mind, I decided.

I resorted to this writing page, the trusted locus of my confessions, my means of investigation of the world. Nothing here is not mine. Well, that may not be true. For a long time, the parliament of censors in my head, my committee of critics, other people's marching orders about what to write and not, how to never reveal secrets, and even the voices of my many nemeses were all here, or they were here most of my life. But I reached the arc of my timidities, my pendulum swung back, and I banished the assassins of my mind.

My only defense against cruelty: writing, literature, the great detoxifier.

The writing page is the only space where being wounded is in fact an advantage. Everywhere else we must wear the mask, sublimate our vulnerability to seem strong, put our best face forward, keep up appearances, or as the Persian idiom goes, *Baa sili soorat-o sorkh negah dashtan*, to keep one's face flush by slapping oneself.

To achieve symmetry, the only option was to make something whose beauty transcended its provenance of brutality. Reinventing the Shamlou opera's narrative meant rewriting my own narrative, it meant owning my story and triumphing over its circumstances. I would have to actively rewire the synapses of my brain to forbid an act of thuggery to derail my life.

It meant not being defined by the event. If the winner of the argument is the one who defines the terms, I redefined the terms. Words steer life, destiny.

In Japan, craftsmen practice the art of *kintsugi*, or "golden joinery," a method of restoring a broken piece with a lacquer that is mixed with gold, silver, or platinum. In Japanese culture, it is important to understand the spiritual background or the history behind the material. This is interwoven with the philosophy of *wabi-sabi*, the concept of finding beauty in broken things or old things. It treats breakage and repair as part of the history of an object, rather than something to disguise. It's not about the broken and fixed item itself, but about the beauty of the person looking at it, about the spiritual life, a beautiful way of living. The broken piece finds a new life as a beautiful art piece. What seemed broken, discarded, useless was transformed into a meaningful gesture.

In 2015, I dreamt that Shamlou was alive. I found him wrapped in a light muslin blanket lying on a bed in a loosely guarded facility of sorts, where he seemed to have volunteered to hide out. I was there too—voluntarily—and had my own room. I had momentary hope that I would simply get his own permission to translate his work. He lets me know that he is aware of what has happened. He seems disappointed, if only half-aware of the whole story. I try to explain. It becomes apparent that the pretense of his death was planned, with everyone in his camp fully complicit. I explain my position, he gets the big picture. The dream then became more about me fixing things in my room. Some of my friends are there.

A close friend, a polymath, interprets the dream: I've moved on to create my own work. The ball is in my court—only my own subconscious is holding me back. I have free rein. The dream suggests that I'm re-vivifying Shamlou. I seek Shamlou's blessing, but he is connected with the very people who hurt me. I entangle him with colleague, who is complicit in his hideaway. A Hideaway, the key turn in this dream. The poet has been rendered invisible by his own estate. When the setting changes to my own room, it suggests that with supporters I am creating something of my own out of the rubble, my own life.

That I had a dream about Shamlou resting in a hospital bed, with some prior but seemingly limited understanding of how his estate ended up censoring me, and by extension, him, that its interpretation is an omen to transcend his hold on me, that our brush with his greatness was fleeting, the magnitude of his legacy intimidating, that we all bear pain in some way or another from his death, that we harbor anxiety over whether we absorbed as much of him—the dead father—as possible, yearning for memories to be restored, that he meant something so personal and inexplicable to us all, that we cannot compute and capture how he shaped and changed our lives, that is the whole knotted magma.

What we do with this brush is the question.

What I do not know is also a form of knowledge. I endow it with wisdom to move me beyond anger. My sole objective is to discover the shape of what I did not yet know, but was always destined to create.

I used to be interested in so many subjects, still am but as my time shrinks I have to retreat within to discover my self because I am a metaphor for the mystery and if I understand my self, that deepest core where I am like everything else, then I will understand the universe, I hope, what other choice do I have, time is escaping and I have yet to write in black and white the results of my expeditions, the sensations are many and I have been a judicious cartographer, now I must connect dots and carve statues. Marguerite Duras says everything is writing, I say that it is only through writing that I survive the brutality of this life.

This book and the opera were how I salvaged the loss. Building something when so much was taken from me. What better place to be than in the catacombs of creation when I am destroyed. Like Shamlou's Abrahams in flames, all those freedom fighters who fought and fell and bled into the earth for their truths, I, too, became a rose.

19. BLOSSOMFIELD

A T THE BEACH I SIT WITH MY BACK UP TO THE BLUFF. I nestle myself tidy and small so as to be shaded on this rare hot day at the ocean while thousands run and splash and heal under the giving sun and do what we have done at the edges of continents for millennia. While I write these sentences, I weep, I have the same intangible feeling of *art* that I had when I first wrote those neat four lines so many years ago.

Put my truth down on paper, no holds barred. This is the organizing principle of my life now, the singular aspiration of my existence. I have no choice, really. There is only me and this blank page. Marguerite Duras wrote that "the person who writes books must always be enveloped by a separation from others. This is one kind of solitude." As difficult as the solitary excavation of pain is from where it goes to be buried, what justifies this self-imposed separation is the fashioning of sweat-blood into meaning, to name the unnamed, to find the unknowable. My struggle is to journey into amorphous recesses, caverns of the hidden self.

This is what I remember reading Rilke had done, "awaiting" his *Duino Elegies*, those otherworldly verses from the hereafter, ushering us to the space beyond our body-bound existence. To stare it—that home we all yearn to return to—in the eye and *poof!* disarm those webs and their hold on our infinity.

In the summer of 2017, my husband and I embarked on a road trip in Europe. We found ourselves in Muggia, a small town along the coast just outside of Trieste, Italy. Not knowing anything about Trieste, I Wikipedia'd it. To my shock, Duino Castle was listed as one of its attractions. Duino! Birthplace of the elegies! Duino! That "cold and damp castle on the Adriatic" where Rilke had sought refuge. Duino, and the meaning it carried for its association with the poems, had for decades occupied a mythical place for me in my mind's eye, something beyond reach akin to Valhalla in the clouds. I actually never thought of it as a real place on this earth. And there it was, a ferry ride and then a bus or bike ride away from my hotel in Muggia! So we went. Even not being much of a cyclist, I pedaled toward it with great ardor up those hills in the muggy heat. When I arrived, dusty and soaked in sweat, I went to the public bathroom, took off my top and shorts in full view, rinsed them in the sink and wrung them. It did not really help to refresh me. But I toured Duino in euphoria, and wet.

It was real. It was open to the public, even if the family that owns it, the von Thurn und Taxis, still occupies a portion of it. It was more like a villa than a castle, which was the ancient structure in semi-ruin very nearby the villa. Rilke had been a guest of Marie von Thurn und Taxis from October 1911 to May 1912 where he wrote major drafts of the first two elegies, the first of which is featured on tourist postcards for sale at the property. *Beauty is only the first touch of terror we can still bear.*

The ticket-seller at the entrance told me that Rilke's rooms were on view, but I could not find one marked as his, even if Rilke memorabilia and photographs were everywhere alongside that of other artists who had stayed at the villa in display cases next to family photos of the von Thurn und Taxis dating a century or so. My husband, seeing that I could not leave the grounds without having seen Rilke's room, asked the groundskeeper about it. He was told the rooms are now occupied by the family, but we were shown a nondescript door up in a remote spiral staircase. I stood there at an unmarked door and quietly wept as my husband snapped photos of a pilgrimage realized.

In late 2013 when I was conceptualizing my Shamlou opera, I was introduced to an opera stage director, Roy Rallo. We immediately began our reveries. I sent him my dossier, and we would meet periodically to dream together. In addition to director, he became dramaturg to the opera, shepherding its metamorphosis. I could not bring myself to tell him for several months about what happened in October 2014. It seemed impossible to articulate the damage. When I did tell Roy, his disquiet was profound: *Don't they realize we are all doing the same thing? Adding to the same work?*

I had originally imagined the opera's libretto to be a composite of extracts from Shamlou's poetry and my own writings. But in light of the hand I had been dealt, everything came to a halt. My budding opera was splintered open. There was a long period of mourning, emptiness, as I could not imagine an opera that was not of Shamlou, devoid of his poetry. Even if I had the rights to translate and publish his poetry, I would not include it in a performance piece. Word by painful word, I expunged his poetry from the libretto, until it was gone. This took months. The disbelief of eliminating his poetry was too difficult to swallow.

In December 2015, Roy and I attended "Forty Part Motet," the Janet Cardiff installation of *Spem in Alium* (Latin for "Hope in Any Other"), Thomas Tallis' forty-part Renaissance motet for eight choirs of five voices each.

Cardiff recorded and calibrated each voice separately and mixed it to allow the audience to hear the piece as we never could otherwise. Each voice was played back through eight clusters of five speakers arranged in a round. The entire work was played in a fourteen-minute loop, eleven minutes of singing with three minutes of intermission. Cardiff added more human touch by leaving microphones on to continue recording as singers spoke, warmed up, mingled before or after their performance.

The installation was in a large, spare gallery space with high ceilings and walls whose upper section was made of glass, opening a view of the sky and tall trees surrounding Fort Mason. The majesty of the trees, the crisp, fresh air of the San Francisco Bay where it meets the Pacific Ocean, the hum of tides, the honesty of the space, the sheer beauty of the music, the proximity and truth in these human voices singing of hope washed away traces of my earthly preoccupations as I sauntered from one speaker to the next, moving at times to the center of the round for the totality to envelop me—it was transformative, spiritual.

My body raced with all kinds of sensations. I dreamt about writing an opera for forty voices, including a chorus and child singers to tell the story of *my* Shamlou. Whereas the opera had always been *about* Shamlou, this was the first time the idea of mirroring entered me— Shamlou as echoed through me. Not *me*, me, as in my stats, but the other me, the reflecting pool of the world, the me that is you, you know, the every*us* me.

Images from Sergei Parajanov's 1969 art film, *The Color of Pomegranates*, the impressionistic journey of the poet-troubadour Sayat Nova's life, told not as a biography, but in a series of *tableaux vivants* depicting scenes and verses from the poet's life, flashed before me. Images of a non-proscenium, immersive opera with audience and singers in close proximity in a sparse and symbolic setting flashed. The music, of utmost importance, would be beautiful, an elegy to the staggering power of art and its succession.

Just as the tornado of sensations was spiraling inside me as I quietly cried facing a corner speaker, I felt Roy come up from behind, put his hand on my shoulder, and himself overcome, tell me that he thought the opera was about *me*, not Shamlou, about how Shamlou had *affected my life*, about the imparting of art, generation to generation.

"Forty Part Motet" and Roy broke my dam of grief, my frozen lake.

Then, as I reimagined the libretto, Aleksandra Vrebalov, who would become the opera's composer in February 2016, remarked that my idealization of Shamlou was a reflection of the artist inside me, projections of my own essence. Something I had never before considered. As my understanding of Shamlou had gradually shifted away from a god-like figure toward a human figure, flaws and all, Aleksandra proposed a feminine poet character for the opera who would serve as a symbolic figure of inspiration and truth, the antithesis of fear and deceit. And Shamlou's tree being shattered by lightning would animate the drama, and the poet would rise from it like a *branch from the forest of the masses*. And the main character of the opera would be sung by a young women's chorus. And the opera would be about the journey and commitment to becoming ourselves, against and through our trials. And it would be called *Abraham in Flames*.

And I would begin to see everything differently, finding the qualities that I shared with Shamlou. I know what you are thinking: *How dare she compare herself to that giant?*

Like Abraham, like Shamlou before me, I am walking through the fire, turning it to rose petals, toppling idols. Human idols, male idols. I am seeing how humans are similar, not different, I am seeing my commitment to my truth, I am becoming me. That's how.

I love a hot sun on my back, I love a clear complexion in the mirror, I love watermelon with feta cheese and walnuts, I love landscapes, I love walking, I love sweating, I love dancing by myself, I love the intimacy of inside jokes, I love that I cry before great paintings, I love relief from tooth pain, I love interrupting "mansplainers," I love people who practice two-way dialogue, I love that some of my orchids bloom again and again because I sure have no control of them, I love that some parts of me are still bourgeois, I love that I can still glide like a swan in heels, I love that I had carefree childhood summers, I love those who gave them to me, I love that I have writing to create my worlds, I love hours well spent, I love eating berries off the vine, I love solitude, I love not feeling alone, I love dreaming that I will be an old artist living on a farm, I love that I have loved and been loved ferociously, I love to make friends laugh at my own expense, I love that I don't have to be right anymore, I love getting older just for that, I love my husband's cousins as my own, I love my constant state of *memento mori*, I love writing this right now, I love my flaws, I love my handful of friends without whom I would be wanting, I love my insistence on what I want despite eye rolls, I love that practicing self-respect is the first step, I love feeling that I am just getting started, I love days without dread, I love my style but I can't afford it, I love my misadventures, I love that I have *this*, this unstoppable, irrational will to create, I love the slippery moment, I love the unbearable potential.

I love that, in time, the Shamlou projects that were stillborn were still born of Shamlou.

CODA

I want to take you back to that frozen image of 1983.

We slowly zoom in on the two standing figures from behind. They are motionless. Only when we arrive up close do we see them breathe. A quivering smile of such slightness sits on their lips. Like the shimmering haze above the span of an ocean that seems to waft into the room. Father and daughter, looking out at the ample neighbor's wife jesting about. The window is tall and French, overlooking their veranda, under which sprawls the garden.

It's the same veranda on which a poet once sat on a summer night to listen to a private recital of Beethoven's *Moonlight Sonata*.

Then the question:

Would you rather be dim and happy or knowing and suffer?

The question seemed to have existed before its utterance, before my existence, before consciousness itself.

Why does my father pick *this* question to ask his young daughter? Were there no other questions, *How many friends will you invite to your birthday party?* Or, *I don't want you talking to the neighbor's son.* Or even, *What do you want to be when you grow up?* But *that* question?

Was it because I happened to be standing there at that moment, viewing a scene that would prompt the question? A prophetic question, before I understood prophetic. Or was I always meant to receive it, my placement next to my father before a jocular scene in that very moment part of the great arc of my life, plunging me t/here.

My suddenly obsolete future flashed before my eyes. Or was it already to be expunged, the question merely a randomly recalled step in that windy path?

Since that moment, nothing has been the same. Decisions were made. Blueprints were sealed. Admission was denied to a lifelong ceremony of the tidy bourgeois mores that I had witnessed. If it were going to be all dinners and showing off jewels and scorn, my parents' very trap that they, too, escaped, it was going to be worthless. I was to be alien, external to the convention.

These primordial memories emerge from the magma of infinite and indefinite time, before our conscious existence. In Persian, the whole of time, an eternity that extends in two directions, is called *abad va azal. Abad* is the eternal future, plus infinity, and *azal* is the eternal past, minus infinity.

The suffering part was a given. Who doesn't suffer? Whole religions are based on the premise of suffering and promise of soothing. Suffering was in the blood. I did not know it then, but later, as an adult I understood the divide between the teachings of my parents. I did not know that I was on a yo-yo ride, trying on one set of parental advice, only to be advised differently by the other. Whose advice would I adopt in my life? Following one seemed like the negation of the other. How would I see the world? Would I follow the values that lead to a knowing life? But what did that mean? Poverty? Did it mean a general melancholy? And the other? To follow the rules, to belong to society. Would that make me happy? Or to live on my own terms, whatever the terms were to be. How would I construct my life? Real rebellion is a journey to the self. The powerless follow.

The suffering my father was referring to was the kind with a capital S. Suffering that undoes beings, the incurable anguish of the depth. Why would I know this at such a young age? And what of the knowing with a capital K? Intuition that cannot be taught, but must source from a well connected by subterranean arms to the spring of Suffering, and yet to the kingdom of Happiness.

Here you are, an artist with a modicum of success, but also a housewife of sorts, nothing like the housewife your mother used to be, before her liberation, for that brand of housewife belongs to a bygone era, for you did voluntarily renounce motherhood, which would have sealed a different destiny, away from your consuming industry. In the darker moments, you strip everything, examine naked facts against the constellation of your hopes and dreams and you secretly wonder whether you did, in fact, take all the wrong steps. But then you snap out of it and realize, *this was not a choice.*

You retrace your steps back to your mother telling you, *Every week I declared English Literature as my major in college, and every week my father would take me by the hand to the university and change it back to Medicine, and so it went and that's how I did not become a doctor and am instead a housewife.* You wonder whether, without intending to, promising yourself that you would never become your mother, you have done as she did, rejected the planned and possibly blazing path. In the end, halfway around the world, decades later, in a new century, your life is somehow superimposed onto hers, or vice versa.

I walk in the woods. The colors are a more vivid version of themselves from behind my sunglasses. The sky is cloudless, a blue blanket. The tall, taupe cypress trunks extend up into the sky. The sun glints off the dark-green cluster of leaves on top. The blue-grey ocean ebbs and flows in a steady, frothy hum. I hear my quick steps on the gravel. Looking up, the vertical lines of the trees against the sky look as if they are passing me by, panel after panel. But it is not them. It is me moving forward, step after step, thought after thought, feeling after feeling, against my time.

Later, I lie on the grass in the breezy, sunny afternoon. The cold fog of San Francisco evenings is imminent. The sky is pure azure blue with scatters of feathery clouds. An airplane crosses my frame. It's unusually visible and corpulent and red. I am wearing a yellow top. Primary colors in the sunlight. By all accounts this is a happy image. The stuff of Peter and Jane and beach balls. But in me runs a low-grade dread of time lost, time not lived, life not actualized, friendships gone, unrestorable, blood ties in crisis and disarray. The anxieties of not only dying but dying tragically, young, of suddenly losing a loved one, of not knowing a single thing about our lives and deaths. Not a single damn thing under the big blue sky.

All the snapshots of the past, the sights and sounds remain shadows, distant, only a few minor steps away from being forever lost. What remains are the echoes of what remains. The composite of blossoming and dying selves. Suppose the four neat lines I jotted down in my notebook, and its accompanying awe that washed over me, and the question of Knowing by the window, were not in fact as eventful as they have been cast by my mind to be. Suppose their importance hinges upon their disproportionate persistence among an ocean of similar, lost memories. Watching snowfall from my bedroom window became the stuff of mythology, the crux of a personal legend, the center of my Creation Story. Would I have been a different person had a different set of my moments been curated and stored in my personal carousel of slides that spin a concocted tale? Would other stories I could tell myself shape a different me, altering everything I had come to build?

The four-line poem was sparse. What was embedded inside those lines that gave it life, lifted it, delivered such mystery, evoking something so unnamable that it transformed me in its birth? And what of the writer? I do not remember having labored over this poem, my first poem. How did the *knowing* form in the distance between watching snowfall and the transcribing? What is at the heart of that alchemical, transportive journey?

We pour ourselves into words, trying our best to express the inexpressible. A Creation Story is nothing but a mandala, a delineation of what is what and how different it is from something else—man, woman, sky, earth, water, tree. We renew language, disassemble and reassemble the patterns of our world ad infinitum to reflect our transforming selves.

Being silenced caused a tectonic shift in me far greater than I imagined. Time allowed me to recast my silencing. It unfurled the me that I am, the me at the window watching snowfall, the me watching the merry wife, the me receiving The Question. My father's question that included in it this very surviving of a crucible, steering me home to a life that had already existed in another dimension, the one I live now.

An undefinable pathos grips me, a whisper of a yearning that I cannot identify. A gossamer on my day, harking from a faraway place. If the senses are not sharp, it goes undetected. But my senses, particularly for elusive filaments, run deep. It dawns on me that I am mourning the ongoing imaginative explosion of my youth. In my mind's eye, it is a GIF of perpetual blossom-burstings, a fireworks of them. I long for the ecstasy of that.

There is wonder everywhere. Yes, all the beautiful things are still here. Wonder now is a honed practice.

I type in my car at the beach to get as much sun as possible in this 70-degree, mid-winter California day. I walk on the beach to catch a last glimpse of the orange orb as it vanishes into the Pacific. The sand flips behind each step and lands copiously into my sneakers. It took the light of the setting sun eight minutes to reach us to register as our passage into night. So what I was seeing was eight minutes in the past. I wonder how we, in these fallible bodies with infinite potential, fit into our own history. I have erased and rewritten myself over and over, and by the time you read this, I will be a phantom to you

a being that was once one thing
but is now another.
Once upon a time
Yeki bood, yeki nabood

Notes

1. Inspired by "The Portrait and the Modern Artist," a broadcast made by Adolph Gottlieb and Mark Rothko on October 13, 1943 on WNYC.

2. David Young, trans. *Duino Elegies:* W.W. Norton & Company, Inc., 1978.

3. Excerpts from *"Grappling with Silence"* by Ahmad Shamlou (from his book, *Unrewarded Eulogies*).

4. Ibid.

5. *"Rupture"* is dedicated to Khosrow Golesorkhi, a poet, journalist, and communist activist who was a Che Guevara–like figure for young Iranians in 1974. During his televised and censored tribunal, he spoke out against the court and was executed for his activism. He asked to forgo the blindfold in order to see the red dawn while singing revolutionary songs. He even called out the order to fire, himself.

6. Excerpt from *"I Searched Among Books,"* a 1981 poem by Ahmad Shamlou (from his book, *Unrewarded Eulogies*).

7. Nasrin Zahiri, *We Came to Visit, You Were Not Home* (Sales, 2014): 79.

8. Excerpt from *"Of Death…",* a December 1962 poem by Ahmad Shamlou (from his book, *Aida in the Mirror*).

9. From William Shakespeare's *Macbeth*.

10. A nocturne (from the French which means nocturnal) is a musical composition inspired by, or evocative of, the night. Shamlou adopted this form for his poetry and coined the term, *shabaneh*, which means nocturnal, but I have translated it back to its (French) origins, nocturne.

11. The term *"rend,"* in the poem, *"An Epic?"* is a complicated concept to translate, without a clear translation in the English language. I translated it as "Fool," a character drawn from the original tarot deck. The concept of *rend* is beyond the scope of these notes, but briefly: The poet Hafez uses *rend* in his poetry to refer to a person who has abandoned social conventions, is outwardly lewd, but inwardly evolved and upright, with a pure heart containing the gem of divine existence within. Summarized from Mohammad Reza Shafiei Kadkani's entry in the Encyclopaedia Iranica: a *rend* is an almost Nietzschean "superman" who reflects the

paradoxical aspects of the human situation, man's free will and predestination, his prayerfulness and rebelliousness, asceticism and besottedness, sorrow and joy. The *rend* is an anti-establishment, counter-culture figure of disrepute, an irreligious alter-ego to Hafez's more reputable persona, a safety valve saving him from the sanctimonious self-righteousness that characterizes the religious authorities.

The Fool occupies the most elevated position in the Tarot de Marseille. He is depicted as a vagabond in rags, almost always unnumbered or labeled the number zero. Alejandro Jodorowsky and Marianne Costa write in their book, *The Way of Tarot: The Spiritual Teacher in the Cards* (Destiny Books, 2009), that they see "the Fool as an individual detached from all needs and complexes and judgments, unbound by any taboos because he has abandoned all demand. He is an illuminatus, a god, a giant drawing an immeasurable liberating strength from the energy flow." Sallie Nichols writes in her book, *Jung and Tarot—An Archetypal Journey,* "The Fool is a wanderer, energetic, ubiquitous, and immortal...Since he has no fixed number, he is free to travel at will, often upsetting the established order with his pranks. His vigor has propelled him across the centuries where he survives in our modern playing cards as the Joker. Here he still enjoys confounding the Establishment..."

12. I was inspired by Samad Alavi's translation in using the word "transfigured."

13. Esfandiar is a legendary hero whose "Achilles' heel" was his eyes.

14. Shamlou uses three cognates of the same root, *nazara* (*n-z-r,* meaning to see, view, watch), to denote stages of engagement in the world and progression toward detachment: *manzar* (a spectacle itself), *nazzaareh* (an engaged spectator), and *naazer* (a detached spectator). To use a trio with similar sounds and avoid having to qualify "spectator," I chose "sport" for the middle phase, which loosely means a person who is engaged in some way.

15. Shamlou meant the "imbecile" addressed in this poem to be Ayatollah Khomeini.

16. From the Afterword by Carlo Jansiti of Violette Leduc's book, *Thérèse and Isabelle,* trans. Sophie Lewis (The Feminist Press at CUNY, 2015).

References

Many books served as inspiration, including: *You Alone are Real to Me* by Lou Andreas Salomé (Trans. Angela von der Lippe), *Glass, Irony and God* by Anne Carson, *Ongoingness* by Sarah Manguso, *The Argonauts* by Maggie Nelson, *The Mother of All Questions* by Rebecca Solnit, *Passenger to Teheran* by Vita Sackville-West, *Writing* by Marguerite Duras (Trans. Mark Polizzotti), *The Waves* by Virginia Woolf, *Don't Let Me Be Lonely: An American Lyric* by Claudia Rankine, *A Tale for the Time Being* by Ruth Ozeki, *White Blight* by Athena Farrokhzad (Trans. Jennifer Hayashida), *Leaving Brooklyn* by Lynne Sharon Schwartz, *An Unnecessary Woman* by Rabih Alameddine, and interviews and essays of Zadie Smith and Ursula K. Le Guin.

Sources consulted for my research include:

Ahmad Shamlou's books printed in Persian

Ahmad Shamlou's Complete Anthology: Books 1 and 2 (Negah, 5th ed., 2004)

The Prince of Tiles by Parvin Salajegheh (Morvarid Publications, 2005)

Bamdad's Mirror: Satire and Epic in Shamlou's Works by Javad Mojabi (Behnegar Publications, 2011)

A Poetic Conversation with Shamlou by Hossein Alizadeh and Seyed Mojtaba Zamiri (Naghsh o Negar, 2001)

We Visited, You Were Not Home by Nassrin Zahiri, (Sales Publication, 2014): 79.

Iranshahr journal, Shamlou issue (Ketab, October 2000, Managing Editor Maliheh Tiregol)

Daftar-e Honar journal, Shamlou issue (ed. Bijan Assadipour, 1997)

"The Poetics of Commitment in Modern Persian: A Case of Three Revolutionary Poets in Iran," a dissertation by Samad Josef Alavi (Autumn 2013)

The Final Word documentary directed by Moslem Mansouri

Ahmad Shamlou, Master Poet of Liberty documentary directed by Moslem Mansouri

The Official Website of Ahmad Shamlou

The A. Bamdad Facebook page

The shamlouhouse Instagram page

The @ShamlouHouse Twitter page

English and Persian Wikipedia

Wikimedia Commons

Encyclopaedia Iranica online

"At Home with Aida Shamlou" (Jadidonline.com, 10/4/2008)

Countless online news and other articles

Shamlou's funeral is reconstructed from anecdotes, blogs, magazine coverage, and photo essays.

I use both Dawn and Daybreak interchangeably as translations of Shamlou's pen name, Alef Bamdad.

Other books of Ahmad Shamlou's poetry in translation:

Born Upon the Dark Spear, Selected Poems of Ahmad Shamlu by Jason Babak Mohaghegh (Contra Mundum Press, December 12, 2015)

The Love Poems of Ahmad Shamlu by Firoozeh Papin-Matin (IBEX Publishers, December 1, 2005)

77 Poems of Ahmad Shamlou by Saeed Saeedpoor (Nika Publication, 2010)

Some dates can vary by one month or one year when converting the Solar Hijri calendar (whose new year begins March 21) to the Gregorian (whose new year begins January 1). They are off by approximately 621 years.

Illustrations

1. Page 23: My snow poem was written in a notebook similar to this one.

2. Page 26: At age three, Tehran, Iran.

3. Page 69: Two of the many tapes my father made me, Tehran, Iran, circa 1982.

4. Page 71: Tehran, Iran, circa 1982.

5. Page 90: Film still from *Poesía Sin Fin (Endless Poetry)* (2017) by Alejandro Jodorowsky. Reproduced by permission from Satori Films.

6. Page 93: Orange County Mehregan Festival, 2006.

7. Page 99: Dr. Eloy Rodriguez and I at a *mercado* in Mexico City, December 1993.

8. Page 102: Iran and its region, courtesy of Google Maps 2018.

9. Page 105: I only recently realized how short the distance was between my home in Behjat Abad and Shamlou's birthplace on Safi Alishah road, District 12, Tehran, Iran. Courtesy of Google Maps 2018.

10. Page 105: My home in Behjat Abad was even closer to south Kheradmand street where Shamlou and Aida had once lived. Courtesy of Google Maps 2018.

11. Page 107: Mount Damavand as a majestic backdrop to Tehran. Damavand Mountain from the Park Sorkhe Hesar. Courtesy of Ninara. https://bit.ly/2Jajga5

12. Page 109: Tehran city limit and its gates, 1848. https://bit.ly/2OHNbN9

13. Page 110: Darvazeh Dowlat (Dowlat city gate), Tehran, Iran. Photograph by Antoin Sevruguin, reprinted by permission from Myron Bement Smith Collection: Antoin Sevruguin Photographs. Freer Gallery of Art and Arthur M. Sackler Gallery Archives. Smithsonian Institution, Washington D.C. Gift of Katherine Dennis Smith, 1973-1985. https://s.si.edu/2yVkz86

14. Page 111: Shahre-farang peep box. https://bit.ly/2R4jimQ

15. Page 150: Mrs. Shamlou's permission letter arrived by email on January 25, 2014.

16. Page 183: Executed prisoner in a public square. Photograph by Antoin Sevruguin. https://s.si.edu/2PkWnql

All personal photographs (#1-4, 6-7, 15) © Niloufar Talebi 2019. No image shall be reproduced.

Acknowledgments

My deepest gratitude to Chris Abani, the best editor I could ask for, Yvette Siegert for blood sisterhood, Christopher Merrill, Russell Scott Valentino, Sam Vaseghi, and Mike Bieker for your support, Farzad Mobin for the cosmic story of *Yeki Bood, Yeki Nabood*, Saied Kazemi for his boundless generosity to me with his time and knowledge of Persian poetry, the late Beryl Joan Fletcher for repeating that I am the real deal, Aria Fani for friendship and scholarly buttressing, Rita Dove for such grace, Roy Rallo for visiting this planet and sharing himself with us, Dr. Maura Williams for supporting my penchant for customized Greek and Latin terms, D.W. Gibson for residencies at the Ledig House, Joshua Robison and Michael Tilson Thomas for a writing sojourn under the much-needed sun, Daniel O'Connell for helping me see some of the translations with new eyes, Zack Rogow, Catherine Parnell, Samantha Schnee, and Richard Jeffrey Newman for literature and friendship, Naheed Attari for all the heart she put into copyediting this book, the beautiful people who still count me a friend despite my occasional vanishings, and Dr. Rafferty who taught me that anxiety is a wasted emotion, and who made space for the literary in our sessions.

My father and mother, the extent of whose love and sacrifice baffles me.

My husband, Donato Cabrera, the sweetness and love of my life.

And Anonymous for supporting my dreams and the writing of this book.

About Ahmad Shamlou

Poet, writer, and translator, Ahmad Shamlou (1925-2000) is widely considered to be one of the most influential cultural figures of modern Iran. He is the author of more than seventy books, a living encyclopedia of Iranian folklore, and numerous translations. He was awarded the Forough Farrokhzad Prize (1973), the Freedom of Expression Award given by Human Rights Watch (1990), the Swedish Stig Dagerman Prize (1999), the Free Word Award given by Poets of All Nations in the Netherlands (2000), and was nominated in 1983 for the Nobel Prize in Literature.

CPSIA information can be obtained
at www.ICGtesting.com
Printed in the USA
LVHW021949280821
696353LV00017B/1895